Whispers from the Land of Snows

Culture-based Violence in Tibet

Whispers from the Land of Snows

Culture-based Violence in Tibet

Fanny Iona Morel

Globethics.net Co-Publications & Other

Director: Prof. Dr Obiora Ike, Executive Director of Globethics.net in Geneva and Professor of Ethics at the Godfrey Okoye University Enugu/Nigeria.

Globethics.net Co-Publications & Other
Fanny Iona Morel, *Whispers from the Land of Snows. Culture-based Violence in Tibet*
Geneva: Globethics.net, 2021
ISBN 978-2-88931-418-8 (online version)
ISBN 978-2-88931-419-5 (print version)
© 2021 Globethics.net

Managing Editor: Ignace Haaz
Cover design: graphism by Michael Cagnoni; photography: Fanny Iona Morel

Globethics.net International Secretariat
150 route de Ferney
1211 Geneva 2, Switzerland
Website: *www.globethics.net/publications*
Email: *publications@globethics.net*

All web links in this text have been verified as of October 2021.

TABLE OF CONTENTS

ACRONYMS

AI	Amnesty International
CCP	Chinese Communist Party
CECC	Congressional-Executive Commission on China
CPPCC	Chinese People's Political Consultative Conference
CRS	Croix-Rouge suisse (Swiss Red Cross)
CTA	Central Tibetan Administration
DIIR	Department of Information and International Relation (CTA)
DwP	Dealing with the Past
FDFA	Federal Department of Foreign Affairs, Switzerland
HRW	Human Rights Watch
ICJ	International Commission of Jurists
ICT	International Campaign for Tibet
IRB	Immigration and Refugee Board of Canada
LIC	Legal Inquiry Committee
MWA	Middle Way Approach
NBSC	National Bureau of Statistic of China
OHCHR	Office of the High Commissioner for Human Rights
PLA	People's Liberation Army

PRC	People's Republic of China
SFA	Swiss Federal Archives
TAR	Tibet Autonomous Region
TCHRD	Tibetan Centre for Human Rights and Democracy
TPSA	Tibetan Policy and Support Act of 2019
TIN	Tibet International Network
UN	United Nations
UDHR	Universal Declaration of Human Rights
UNPO	Unrepresented Nations & Peoples Organization
USDOS	US Department of State

ACKNOWLEDGEMENTS

This study was conducted within the framework of the project *Respect for Cultural Rights and Prevention of Violence* of the Observatory of Diversity and Cultural Rights, based at the Interdisciplinary Institute of Ethics and Human Rights of the University of Fribourg, Switzerland. I received invaluable advice and encouragement from several people, who kindly shared their wealth of knowledge and experience. Without their valuable support, this study would not have been possible. Much of the essential information comes from interviewees and sources who requested anonymity. Thus, I would like to thank these individuals above all for generously sharing their stories and points of view with me, as well as for enriching this publication with their drawings, photographs and documentation. I am sincerely grateful for the trust and time they have given me. Special thanks are due to Shede Dawa: I owe him a great deal for his availability and support. My sincere thanks also go to Golok Jigme for the valuable information he provided, as well as to Migmar Dhakyel, who made our meeting possible and agreed to be our interpreter. I am likewise grateful to Tsering Wangdu for taking the time to talk to me during his solo peace march across Switzerland (May–June 2020).

I would like to express my sincere gratitude to Dr. Patrice Meyer-Bisch who supported me from the very beginning and provided me with the opportunity to carry out this long-planned project. His expertise was invaluable at every stage of my work. I would also like to acknowledge Dr Greta Balliu and Johanne Bouchard for their insightful comments, and Dr Emilia Sulek for sharing with me her vast knowledge about Tibetan nomads. Outside academia, I would like to thank the Tibet Bureau (Geneva), Tenzin Wangmo, Thomas Büchli and René Longet from the Swiss-Tibetan Friendship Association, René Canzali from ACAT-Suisse, and NGOs that wished to remain anonymous. I would also like to thank Roland Böhlen, an archivist and historian at the Red Cross Switzerland, Bern, and Laurent Mousson, the documentation and publications manager for Amnesty International, Bern. Last but not least, I am sincerely grateful to my family and friends for their invaluable moral support.

F. I. Morel

INTRODUCTION

The outcome of the absolute authority exercised by the People's Republic of China (PRC) in Tibet is of great concern. Since 1949, Tibetans – both as individuals and as a community – have been subject to widespread human rights violations and uncertainty regarding their future. In 2008, Tibetans stood up on a massive scale for their rights and freedoms for the last time, as the world prepared to celebrate the Summer Olympics in Beijing. Following their plea for help to the international community, Tibetans and Tibet itself were further walled in with silence, as repression[1] intensified. Tibetans continue to strive for their right to exist as fully fledged individuals and to express their cultural identity without fear of persecution. Thus, the promotion and enforcement of cultural rights concern the safety and well-being of individuals, going well beyond the protection of cultural property. The Tibetan question must be understood to concern an urgent effort to guarantee respect for Tibetans' rights and freedoms in Tibet, as well as their immediate protection and relief, and to provide a basis for a peaceful future for Tibetans – whether in Tibet itself or in exile – as well as for the PRC. Countries that grant

---

[1] "Repression refers to government policies in which force and threats are widely used to restrict the movement and political   activities of members of a minority or national people." p. 272 Charney, Israel W. 1999: Encyclopedia of Genocide Volume I & II, ABC-CLIO, Santa Barbara.

asylum to Tibetans are de facto involved in the Tibet issue. Violations of international human rights law cannot be ignored under the pretext of respecting PRC's domestic laws and affairs. The Tibetan question is a systemic problem affecting Tibetans and their host countries, across the globe. In this regard, the violations of human rights in Tibet are a transnational issue, one that cannot be considered as a mere internal matter for the PRC.

This study is dedicated to stories from Tibet that have reached another land of snows, Switzerland. It is the result of initial interdisciplinary research, essentially conducted on the basis of the testimonies of exiled Tibetans. This material was supplemented by the testimony of witnesses and sources from different nationalities, as well as by my own observations in the Tibet Autonomous Region (TAR) in 2019. The collected narratives reveal the living conditions of Tibetans under Chinese rule, showing their attachment to their faith, values and environment, both natural and cultural. More specifically, they underline the central cultural element in the violence perpetrated against Tibetans in Tibet. Early in the research project, narratives presented by Tibetan interviewees emphasised that, although the preservation of their cultural identity was of central importance, their priority was, above all, survival and the need for security. In the present situation, Tibetans seeking a minimum level of safety must comply with Chinese rules. These testimonies gave voice to a very painful abandonment of faith, values, dignity and freedoms, which still does not exempt Tibetans from discrimination and suspicion on the part of Chinese authorities. Their safety, therefore, remains precarious, whatever path they consider most appropriate. Witnesses expressed their unease about the prospects for their physical and cultural survival, both as individual and as community members, in the face of the repressive and assimilationist measures that the PRC has implemented in Tibet for decades now. Overall, the testimonies articulate Tibetans' aspirations for a peaceful future, where peace can be defined in terms of respect for one's dignity and well-being, rather than the mere absence of war (UN NEWS 2021). Peace, in this sense, is compromised when real or perceived grievances arise and are not addressed by the state. As such, safety, in the sense of an absence of indiscriminate violence, is not guaranteed in Tibet. Within the framework of this study, the focus was on violations of human rights and civil freedoms, and more particularly on cultural identity issues. Although this study applies the concept of genocide elaborated by Raphael Lemkin, a historian and international law specialist (1900–1959), the 1948 Convention on the Prevention and Punishment of the Crime of Genocide (Appendix A) remains the primary source of law. This study also makes extensive use of the 2007 Declaration on the Rights of Indigenous Peoples (Appendix B) and of Articles 3 and 4 on cultural identity and cultural community of the 2007 Fribourg Declaration on Cultural Rights (Appendix C). The latter text develops and supplements the critical points regarding cultural rights raised by international human rights legislation, which refer to the rights of individuals and communities to safely and freely choose and express their cultural identity.[2] The approach adopted in this study aims to identify several cases that show the genocidal nature of the violations of cultural identity rights in Tibet.

It is impossible to dictate someone else's cultural references. The existence of a unique and uncompromising identity is not only illusory, but trying to impose one promotes violence (SEN 2006:175). Every individual has their own unique cultural identity that evolves with their experiences, making the past an essential ingredient in diversity. Expressions of cultural identities strengthen feelings of belonging and are a source of pride. The need to protect, share and transmit them to future generations is, therefore, legitimate, as well as being essential for promoting mutual understanding, tolerance and dialogue between individuals and commu-

---

[2] The definitions of culture, cultural identity and community used in this work are taken from Article 2 of the Fribourg Declaration.

nities with different worldviews. Moreover, knowing about the past is important when it comes to fighting against the impunity of perpetrators who commit abuses on the behalf of their government and preventing their recurrence. Acknowledging atrocities and establishing the circumstances under which violations of human rights have occurred is an inalienable responsibility of a state, whose function is to restore the dignity of victims and prevent the recurrence of violence (FDFA 2018; SWISSPEACE 2016:6). Tibetans living in Tibet should be entitled to access and share information regarding the past, as well as to give their free, prior and informed consent and to be involved in the decision-making processes impacting their way of life, their history and their future (UN A/HRC/39/62 2018). Yet, Tibetans have suffered mass violence, which has been perpetrated with impunity, and continue to be subjected to severe human rights violations. In 1960, the Legal Committee for the Investigation of the Question of Tibet stated that acts of genocide had been perpetrated in Tibet by the PLA. With regard to current events, the Tibet Autonomous Region is reported to have been the "testing ground for many of the techniques now used in Xinjiang" against Uighurs and members of other Muslim minorities (US Senate Committee on Foreign Relations 2018:3). In 2021, Tibet was also ranked as the world's least free territory by Freedom House, tied with Syria (Freedom House 2021). The repression exercised against Tibetans, while constantly changing and of variable intensity, has caused and continues to cause a significant human death toll, profound suffering and a pervasive sense of insecurity in Tibet.

In addition to laying out the definitions and methods used, the first chapter will explain how the testimonies were collected and analysed. Chapter 2 will summarise key historical events that have led to violence and endangered Tibetans, both as individuals and as a community, since the PLA entered Eastern Tibet in 1949. The history of the Chinese occupation is one marked by deadly events, including the Great Leap Forward (1958–1962), the Cultural Revolution (1966–1976)[3] and three major Tibetan uprisings (in 1959, 1987–1989 and 2008). This chapter will also focus on the atrocity crimes committed in Tibet, revisiting the official definition of genocide and developing it with reference to Lemkin's concept. In the following chapters, the cultural component of violence in Tibet will be examined in more depth. Prevented from freely enjoying their cultural identity – and particularly their faith – Tibetans expressed their fear, distress and dismay at the ongoing violence in Tibet, which affects monasticism, education, the Tibetan language and nomadism, as will be seen in Chapter 3. The right of Tibetans to learn about their own history, as well as about the past and current abuses they have suffered, were also amongst the main concerns for the interviewees. Chapter 4 will thus look at how the denial of violence and the manipulation of the history of Tibet by the Chinese Communist Party (CCP) impedes the healing process of survivors of abuse and of victims' families. It will also address the CCP's willingness to undermine the moral influence exercised on Tibetans by Tibet's spiritual leader and historic figure, the 14th Dalai Lama (born in 1935), while seeking to replace him. This study focuses on the violence suffered by Tibetans, but it also recounts acts of protest and resilience. Self-immolations are a sensitive topic that were discussed several times during the interviews. Chapter 5 will relate the desperation of Tibetans who resort to such extreme self-harm, but will also examine Tibetans' power of resiliency and opportunities for peace. The situation in Tibet is complex and rapidly evolving. Against this backdrop, the present study represents a modest contribution to the Tibetan question, which, without claiming to be exhaustive, seeks to be comprehensive. The issues related here need – and deserve – more in-depth research. If the effects that this study will have are, for now, unpredictable, I hope it will contribute to the promo-

---

[3] Officially from 1966 until 1976, the year of Mao Zedong's death. Violence and exactions continued in Tibet until 1979.

tion of more initiatives dealing with human rights violations, so as to promote peacebuilding and the prosperity of peoples living under the stranglehold of authoritarian regimes.

> *A new era is coming for China they [the CCP] say. But who is it good for? Good for Han Chinese? And what about Tibetans?* (Interview #10)

1

METHODOLOGY:
THE VOICE OF TIBETANS

Introduction

Collaboration with Tibetans was at the heart of the participative approach adopted in this interdisciplinary study. Interviews were essential for obtaining access to uncensored information, as well as for learning more about the experiences and perceptions of Tibetans who have lived in Tibet, most of whom have suffered from various forms of violence and were forced to flee. First and foremost, it was necessary to define Tibet geographically, as the legal definition connected to the Tibetan Autonomous Region did not reflect the participants' own views about the matter. This chapter also explains the difficulties involved in gaining access to Tibet, especially the TAR, and in obtaining first-hand information. Given that human rights violations in Tibet are a highly sensitive topic, a conflict-sensitive approach was indispensable. Several measures were taken to ensure both the confidentiality of the participants' personal data and their anonymity, in order to prevent retaliations against their relatives and contacts in Tibet.

Ethnic unity and China's Tibet. A law on ethnic unity in the TAR took effect on 1 May 2020. Tibetans have the legal obligation "to safeguard national reunification, strengthen ethnic unity and take a clear-cut stand against separatism." (YUWEI 2020). *Morel, Gawula Pass, TAR, 2019.*

1.1 Tibet and China's Tibet

There is no unambiguous and straightforward way of defining Tibet. The interpretations of and vocabulary used to refer to Tibet and its former territories vary according to the perspective chosen, whether geographical, cultural, historical or political. There are, however, two main definitions. For the Central Tibetan Administration (CTA), Tibet corresponds to Ü-Tsang, Amdo and Kham. And in fact, the witnesses always referred to the former names of the Tibetan territories. For the CCP, by contrast, Tibet is the Tibet Autonomous Region (TAR), formalised by the Party in 1965 and recognised internationally. The change of name suited the vocabulary of the PRC, making Tibet a Chinese autonomous region. However, in the TAR, just as in the PRC as whole, the political system remains dominated by Han Chinese, and the role of Tibetans is reported to be largely symbolic (Freedom House 2021). The TAR is restricted to Ü-Tsang and Western Kham, but neither Tibetan name is officially used by the PRC. Only the TAR matters. Amdo was integrated into the Chinese provinces of Qinghai, Gansu and Sichuan, while Eastern Kham, merged into Qinghai, Sichuan, and Yunnan. The definition of Tibet given by participants (Tibetans and foreigners alike) correlated with that of the CTA. Consequently, it is this definition of Tibet that will be used in the following. Despite a lack of reliable sources, the Tibetan population in Tibet in 2018 was estimated to be around 6 million, compared to 7.5 million Han Chinese. In the TAR, Tibetans numbered 2.62 million, representing 93% of the population (UNPO 2018). The majority of the Tibetan population in the PRC practices Mahayana Buddhism, with minorities practicing Bon, Islam, Catholicism or Protestantism (US DOS 19 June 2019).

The PRC considers Tibet a sensitive region and maintains tight control over the territory and its population. Restrictions on Tibetans' freedom of movement, especially to and within the TAR, have been reported and will be further discussed in Chapter 2. Access to Tibet is also limited for foreigners, if not blocked entirely. The movements of foreign visitors are also controlled and monitored, preventing fact-finding missions and investigation into human rights violations against Tibetans (Observations # 15; Freedom House 2021). Since 2008, the borders of the TAR are closed at least once a year, from February to March (TCHRD 2020:23). These months correspond, respectively, to the Tibetan *Losar*, or New Year's festival, and to the 1959 Tibetan uprising, which is commemorated every year on 10 March across the globe by the Tibetan diaspora. The PRC can also – sporadically and with short notice – deny access to the TAR to foreigners at any time of the year. A source in Nepal explains that border closures do not necessarily affect Han Chinese, recounting the recent case of the reopening of the TAR in summer 2020, after the COVID-19 pandemic lockdown. While Han

Chinese tourists were once again authorised to travel to the TAR, foreigners were still banned, even holders of permanent-resident status in the PRC. The documents required to travel to and within Tibet vary according to the area. For instance, in order to access the TAR, foreigners must first register with an official local Tibetan or Chinese tourist agency and join a guided tour approved in advance by the Chinese authorities. This step is mandatory in order to acquire a Tibet Entry Permit (access from the PRC) or a Group Tourist Visa (access from Nepal). Further permits can be required for specific areas and cultural sites. Travellers are constantly accompanied by accredited Tibetan or Chinese guides and drivers. The compliance of both guides and visitors with the terms of tourist circuits is monitored. Thus, the rhythm of travel through the TAR is governed by numerous security checkpoints and passport controls. Foreigners only enjoy a certain degree of freedom, when going for a walk in towns and cities, but even then, they must keep their passport on them for identity checks (Observations #15). Although a Chinese visa is sufficient for gaining access to Tibetan regions outside the TAR, foreigners still face restrictions, monitoring and forbidden areas (Interview #6; Freedom House 2021). Since the government also controls media and censors competing information, Tibetans have minimal contact, if any at all, with the outside world. That said, restrictions on access to Tibet and the high level of scrutiny from Chinese authorities should not discourage foreign travellers. Visiting Tibet is essential to avoid its complete isolation from the outside world. Furthermore, every visitor can potentially be a valuable source of information for human rights investigations and advocacy. Amongst the Tibetans interviewed, several spontaneously declared that they were happy to learn that Westerners were still going to Tibet, not only on the grounds that these Westerners would "see what's happening with their own eyes" (Interview #21), but also simply because the interviewees are proud of their land.

1.2 Religious Freedom: A Legal Right

Religious freedom is a fundamental, protected right. Article 18 of the Universal Declaration of Human Rights (UDHR) states that every individual has the right to enjoy religious freedom. Religious freedom is intertwined with other fundamental rights, notably the right to freedom of expression and opinion, as well as the right to freedom of association. It also entails the right to non-discrimination and equality for all. No one may be compelled to declare non-adherence to religious belief in order to obtain employment and social or economic benefits (WALSH 2024:2–3, 7). As Article 30 recalls, "[n]othing in this Declaration may be interpreted as implying for any State, group or person any right to engage in any activity or to perform any act aimed at the destruction of any of the rights and freedoms set forth herein."

The PRC is signatory of the UDHR, but its interpretation of religious freedom potentially differs from that of the UDHR. In the Constitution of the People's Republic of China, religious freedom is guaranteed by Article 36, but it specifies that the country "protects normal religious activities", without making clear what "normal" implies (USDOS 12 May 2021). It states that religion may not be used to engage in "activities that disrupt public order" and that "[r]eligious bodies and religious affairs are not subject to any foreign domination." Buddhism counts amongst the five official religions recognised by the state, along with Taoism, Islam, Protestantism and Catholicism. Religious figures, activities, and sites must be registered, regulated and approved by the authorities from the Religious Affairs Bureau in order to acquire legal status, thus restricting religious freedom (CECC 2010:214; APPLEBY 2000:209; WALSH 2014:9). Yet, religious figures and worshippers are still confronted with persecution, monitoring, discrimination and marginalisation (Interviews #1, #3, #8, #14, #19, #20, #21, #22; USDOS 12 May 2021). The 2005 Regulation on Religious Affairs was supplemented by several measures to create an 'order' for Tibetan Buddhism (CECC 2010:220–221). The PRC's utilitarian view of Buddhism is expressed by the CCP's policies to restrict access to monasteries, spiritual education and practices, its appointing of religious leaders and its pervasive interference in religious affairs (APPPLEBY 2000:209; CSW 2021). Moreover, laws criminally sanction non-registered Buddhist religious activities and limit forms of religious expression deemed a threat to national security, thus constituting "draconian methods" for repressing religious freedom (WALSCH 2014:10–11).

1.3 Sources and Interviews

Background research was undertaken before my trip to the TAR in 2019 and the interviews started upon my return. Both primary and secondary sources were collected and studied, including UN and NGO reports and documentation, archives and academic publications. This project led me to identify the central role of cultural rights for Tibetans and highlighted the need to concentrate on the cultural element and contributing factors that could trigger violence. Due to the delicacy of the issue, a conflict-sensitive approach was necessary. The Tibetans who participated in this study were nuns, monks, nomads, farmers, teachers or artists who had escaped persecution or fled from a "life that had become soul-crushing" (Interview #18). Despite their willingness to speak out, their priority was the safety of their loved ones still in Tibet. It was therefore essential to protect their anonymity. Only two Tibetan interviewees, the monk Golok Jigme and Tsering Wangdu, both of whom are human rights activists, agreed to reveal their identities. Other sources also demanded confidentiality, for fear of retaliation against their contacts in Tibet. Under Chinese law, it is a crime to communicate information and opinions to foreigners that might conflict with the CCP's propaganda, such as about human rights violations (TIN 1997:viii). Conducting face-to-face interviews, especially with exiled Tibetans, thus required time so as to build genuine reciprocal trust. Our collaboration started in 2016. With the help of other volunteers, we organised cultural events and activities in Switzerland to strengthen mutual understanding between our cultures. It was only in 2019 that the participants and I agreed to collaborate on a new project focusing on human rights issues in Tibet. Interviews took place all across Switzerland, in locations agreed at the last moment with the interviewees. Three Tibetans accepted to interpret from Tibetan into English or French. Their participation was doubly valuable, since they were competent and their presence reassured their fellow Tibetans, who decided to participate in this research project. Altogether, 23 people were interviewed, mostly between October 2019 and July 2020. All Tibetan interviewees were born in Tibet (Kham, 10; U-Tsang, 7; Amdo, 2) and had extensive experience in their homeland. Most of them had arrived in Europe after the events of 2008. They all indicated that they were Buddhists and devoted to the Dalai Lama. Consequently, their beliefs, faith and values occupied an important place during the interviews and when discussing the violations of cultural rights in Tibet. The remaining four interviewees were foreign nationals who had lived in Tibet for at least a year or had close ties with locals.

To this, I added my own observations, made during my trip to Tibet (TAR) in 2019. I also benefited from the support of 11 sources (Nepal: 4, Europe: 7), who were not interviewed, but who provided information, documents and most of the photographs published here. Furthermore, specific material on Tibet and cultural rights issues was shared by the Observatory of Diversity and Cultural Rights, the Tibet Bureau (Geneva), the Swiss-Tibetan Friendship Association, ACAT-Suisse and NGOs that wished to remain anonymous. Interviews with Tibetans were open discussions, semi-structured with open-ended questions and adapted to the interviewees' occupation before their exile.

In the case of the foreign interviewees, interviews were either semi-structured or structured, with open-ended questions. It was essential for interviewees, especially Tibetans, not to feel any pressure to talk about subjects that were too sensitive or personal. It was important not to jeopardise their relatives' safety and to avoid mentioning events that could be too painful for them to recount. Furthermore, open-ended questions allowed them to share their opinions, perceptions and feelings, which were just as important. The interviews were neither filmed nor recorded. Instead, the testimonies were directly transcribed during our discussions and made identifiable by means of a number, the date and location of the interview and, where possible, by the interviewee's former occupation and origin (U-Tsang, Amdo, Kham, or country). Interviews took between one and three hours. In every case, interviewees had the opportunity to either add or withdraw information after the interview. It was necessary to keep in contact with them all through the duration of this study, in order to ensure the continuous validation of data and to enable clarifications about specific questions and discussions. The Tibetan interviewees had no vested interest in participating in this work, as I have no involvement in asylum procedures. These testimonies were collected exclusively for this study. They were not and will not ever be shared with any third party.

The interviews all took place between October 2019 and June 2020, with a break during the Covid-19 pandemic lockdown in March and April. Tibetan interviewees' former occupations in Tibet are mentioned where relevant. For foreigners, only their area of expertise is specified.

Interview#	Date of interview	Place of origin	Occupation
Interview #1	11/10/2019	Kham	Teacher
Interview #2	22/10/2019	U-Tsang	Nomad
Interview #3	29/10/2019	Kham	Monk
Interview #4	29/10/2019	Kham	Farmer
Interview #5	29/12/2017	Switzerland	Unspecified
Interview #6	02/02/2018	Switzerland	Unspecified
Interview #7	05/11/2019	Kham	Unspecified
Interview #8	21/11/2019	U-Tsang	Nomad, farmer, then monk
Interview #9	22/11/2019	U-Tsang	Unspecified
Interview #10	26/11/2019	Kham	Self-employed
Interview #11	29/11/2019	Kham	Nomad
Interview #12	03/12/2019	Amdo	Nomad
Interview #13	05/12/2019	Kham	Nomad and farmer
Interview #14	12/12/2019	U-Tsang	Monk
Observations TAR #15	09/2019 Field observation	-	-
Interview #16	16/12/2019	Switzerland	Human rights
Interview #17	17/12/2019	Switzerland	Education
Interview #18	18/12/2019	Kham	Artist
Interview #19	02/01/2020	U-Tsang	Nomad
Interview #20	02/01/2020	Kham	Monk
Interview #21 Tsering Wangdu	02/06/2020	Kham	Labourer
Interview #22	20/06/2020	U-Tsang	Monk
Interview #23 Golok Jigme	24/06/2020	Amdo	Monk
Interview #24	28/06/2020	U-Tsang	Nun

1.4 Analysis of Testimonies

We have a lot of problems and many things to say. We suffer, but we can't give too many details because it's risky for our families. (Interview #20)

The possibility of systematically fact-checking the collected statements and reported events was limited as a result of the lack of access to uncensored information from Tibet. However, the consistency of the testimonies, the reasonableness of the facts alleged and their coherence with common knowledge and previous research of the context helped when it came to assessing the credibility of the claims being made. After an initial analysis of the data collected, common patterns were identified and coded with reference to five key fields significantly affected by cultural rights violations and violence: monastic life, language, education, nomads/environment (Chapter 3) and history (Chapter 4). First of all, as a highly spiritual land, the Party's authority over Buddhist affairs in Tibet was expected to be a significant concern. The testimonies underline the moral suffering of nuns and monks and recounted peaceful protests that were suppressed with violence. Restrictions on educational opportunities were mentioned regularly, as were the patriotic re-education campaigns that affect all Tibetans, children as well as adults (CECC 2020:2). The preservation of the Tibetan language is another prime concern for Tibetan witnesses. The interviews notably highlighted the indivisibility of the protection of the Tibetan language from the preservation of Tibetan knowledge. Nomadism and monasticism are considered the last representatives and repositories of authentic Tibetan culture. However, both ways of life are endangered. Nomads, in particular, increasingly suffer from financial burdens and can be forced to settle in villages or cities. Last but not least, the Tibetan interviewees were firmly committed to talking about their version of Tibet's history and the system-wide impunity in the PRC with respect to past atrocities and ongoing severe human rights violations. They shared their distress at the repressive measures taken against spiritual leaders, in particular against the Dalai Lama and against the 11th Panchen Lama (born in 1989, enforced disappearance in 1995). The foreign interviewees all talked about at least one of these common themes. They testified to the suffocating atmosphere of oppression imposed on Tibet by the PRC. They reported Tibetans' disarray at seeing their rights systematically violated, their suffering, fear, and overall struggle silenced by the CCP.

Conclusion

A credibility assessment was conducted whenever possible, depending on the availability of uncensored information from Tibet. The testimonies were, on the whole, coherent, plausible and consistent with the background research. The benefit of the doubt was granted to claims and facts for which there were no supporting information or sources. Interviewees had no personal interest in participating in this study and the requisite confidentiality and anonymity should not be seen as undermining the reliability of the testimonies. The interviewees' fear of retaliation is real and, as such, must be taken into account. It indicates the seriousness of the widespread and ongoing insecurity perceived in Tibet. If the PRC were beyond reproach in the area of human rights, such strict control and monitoring would be unnecessary and disproportionate.

2

THE DRAGON'S RED FLAG

Tibet has suffered much during the years of Chinese Communist Party rule, as has all of the People's Republic of China. But Tibet's cultural and religious life has been more severely attacked by the Communist Party than the tradition of the Han culture. Still, Tibetan culture has managed to survive; it seems to have great resilience. (LIZHI 2015:37)

Introduction

The human rights and security developments that have taken place in Tibet since the Chinese takeover have not benefited Tibetans. The territory has been marked by violence that has endangered them, both individually and as a community. Although the situation seemed to have eased in the 1980s, violence resumed at the end of the decade. The repression increased in scale, but also adopted a more insidious form that shielded it from the glare of attention from both the Chinese public and the international community. Witnesses report persecutions, the mass surveillance of public spaces, interference in the private sphere of Tibetans and reprisals against anyone perceived to be rejecting the CCP's authority. Several witnesses even compare the Tibet Autonomous Region to an open-air prison. This chapter will summarise the major events that have occurred since 1949, using testimonies of the current situation in Tibet. It will also recall that the acts of genocide perpetrated against

Tibetans (ICL 1960:17), widespread impunity and severe, ongoing human rights violations (USDOS 2021; TCHRD 2020) are the breeding grounds for further atrocity crimes in Tibet. Lemkin's concept of genocide will also be detailed, since it provides insights into the devastating consequences of policies aimed at repressing every aspect of Tibetan society. Lemkin not only focuses on the partial or total biological elimination of oppressed peoples, he also explains how the oppressor's coordinated actions may lead to the eradication of the essential foundations of the national identity[4] of the oppressed people (LEMKIN 1944:79).

2.1 Recalling Violence: Takeover and Stranglehold

In September 1949, the Chinese People's Political Consultative Conference (CPPCC) adopted the so-called "Common Program", which established equal rights and obligations for all ethnic groups in the PRC. It guaranteed that the state would always apply a policy of ethnic equality, unity, regional autonomy and religious freedom (QINGYING 2004:112). That same year, not long after the proclamation of the PRC by Mao Zedong (1893–1976), the PLA entered Eastern Tibet, to enact what is still called the "Peaceful Liberation of Tibet" by the PRC. The army defeated Tibetan forces at the Battle of Chamdo, or Qamdo (Kham), on 6–19 October 1950, before marching on Lhasa. Under military pressure, a Tibetan government delegation was sent to Beijing to negotiate. The Seventeen-Point Plan for the Peaceful Liberation of Tibet (Appendix D), also known as the "17-Point Agreement", was signed under duress on 23 May 1951 by the Tibetan government, with conditions imposed by their Chinese counterparts (BUFFETRILLE/RAMBLE 1998:7). The PRC claimed Tibet as a Chinese territory, and this claim statement was sealed with a written document (Point 1). The agreement

---

[4] Lemkin points out that the notion of nation should not be confused with that of nationalism (LEMKIN 1944:91).

promised Tibetans that their religion, language and educational practices would be respected (Points 7 and 9). It also assured them that reforms would not be imposed on Tibet (Point 11). However, the realities of the Chinese occupation faced by Tibetans stood in stark contrast to the terms of the agreement. Monasteries were looted, damaged or destroyed, their authority was usurped and they were forced to cooperate with the Party. In 1953, the latter created the Buddhist Association of China as a means of enforcing its jurisdiction over Buddhist affairs. Eastern Tibet, namely Kham and Amdo, was at the frontline of the Chinese takeover, as well as of Tibetan resistance. Revolts occurred as early as 1952–1953 (NORBU 1979:82), while significant uprisings emerged in Kham in 1955/1956 and Amdo in 1958 (NORBU 1979:84). The PLA moved to suppress the resistance, spreading terror amongst the population. Fleeing persecution, thousands of Tibetans sought refuge in the Lhasa area. Widespread fear and tensions increased, reaching a climax with the 1959 Tibetan uprising in Lhasa, which resulted in the heavy loss of Tibetan lives, in addition to significant suffering and mass exile, including that of the 14th Dalai Lama. The exile of nuns and monks fleeing persecution contributed to an exodus of ancestral knowledge. The killings and destruction of cultural wealth essentially occurred in monasteries (ICJ 1959:36–37).

That same year, the International Commission of Jurists (ICJ) voiced concerns regarding the Chinese takeover of Tibet and the brutality endured by Tibetans. The report warns that what "appears to be attempted genocide may become the full act of genocide unless prompt and adequate action is taken." (ICJ 1959:71). Notably, the ICJ expressed the view that Articles 2a and 2e of the 1948 Convention for the Prevention and Punishment of Genocide had been violated. Furthermore, the events related by the Dalai Lama and other Tibetan witnesses provided evidence of "a systematic intention by such acts and other acts to destroy in whole or in part the Tibetans as a separate nation and the Buddhist religion in Tibet." (ICJ 1959:71). In a report issued in 1960, however, the Legal Inquiry Committee (LIC) concluded that the mass violence suffered by the Tibetan population could not be recognised as genocide, on the grounds that there was a lack of sufficient evidence (LIC 1960:17). Still, the LIC admitted that individual acts of genocide had been perpetrated in Tibet (LIC 1960:17) and stressed the deprivation of Tibetans' religious freedom. In 1960, Chinese radio announced the execution of 87,000 Tibetans by the PLA, in and around Lhasa (KOPF 1999:543). Additionally, the 10th Panchen Lama (1949–1989) stated that, in the wake of the 1959 uprising, 110,000 monks (out of 600,000) died following persecutions, while a further 250,000 were forced to return to secular life (ZILIN/PEIKUN 2015:31). Killings in Tibet were arguably directed at particular strata of Tibetan society, e.g. influential personalities and religious figures, who were considered class enemies. As Margolin states, however, there were periodic shifts in the groups targeted. In the PRC and Tibet, individuals who came to be considered the new adversaries of the CCP did not replace earlier targeted groups, but were simply added to them (MARGOLIN 2008:438). Consequently, every Tibetan became a potential enemy of the PRC. According to the CTA, more than 1.2 million Tibetans in total died of unnatural causes under Chinese rule. The exact number of casualties amongst Tibetans is unknown, but significant loss of life from unnatural causes following the Chinese invasion is undeniable (BARNETT 2008:89). Moreover, testimonies collected for this study underline that an unknown number of Tibetans were, and still are, victims of enforced disappearances, humiliation, torture – along with other cruel, inhumane or degrading treatments or punishments (USDOS 2021) – and exhausting forced labour in factories, farms or construction sites. The whereabouts of the disappeared in many cases remains unknown or their fate is shrouded in silence, even by Tibetans themselves out of fear of reprisals (Interviews #1, #9, #21, #23, #24).

In Tehor [Drago district, Kham], before the Chinese occupation, about 1,000 monks lived in various monasteries. Most were destroyed during the Cultural Revolution, but some were rebuilt or restored by Tibetans by their own means in the 1980s. If China took care of some of them, it was under their conditions. The Chinese reduced the capacity of monasteries and changed their appearances. (Interview #1)

1/3 - Lhasa and Tibet before the occupation, as depicted by the artist. Lhasa was luxurious, especially Norbulingka Palace. There were lakes and bamboo. After the Chinese takeover, the clouds watched over the Tibetans and prevented them from moving freely, as illustrated here by means of the numerous clouds on the path leading to a tree and a mountain, symbolising Tibet, and more specifically the degradation of its environment. From the 1980s, the sun, or the world, started real-ising the severity of the situation, even if only partially. *Anonymous Tibetan artist, Switzerland, 2020.*

2/3 - The artist depicts here the Chinese invasion of Tibet in 1949. The clouds represent the PRC, which prevents Tibetans from con-templating the sky. They thus symbolise Tibetans' lack of freedom and the oppression they endure. The clouds also hide the violence and torture in Tibet from the rest of the world, depicted here by a far-away sun. With the tree and rocks, the artist hopes to alert the world to Tibet's environmental degradation since the Chinese takeover. The flowers on the ornamental frieze represent, on the other hand, his hope for world peace. *Anonymous Tibetan artist, Switzerland 2020.*

In our area, people who do politics [activists] disappear at night, in secret. They might be sentenced to life in prison, but nobody knows. Also, in our remote village, there was a monastery, but it remained empty for years. Monks weren't allowed to stay there. After 2005, it changed and about 20 monks lived in the monastery, but they were under a lot of restrictions and the authorities put pictures of the Chinese leaders in the monastery. (Interview #19)

Our monastery was destroyed during the Cultural Revolution. We got together to rebuild it, thanks to private donations from Tibetans. It took us two years. Once built, the Chinese government sent collaborators to our monastery, as if it belonged to them. They came to instill their ideology, their laws, their rules on the nuns. We had to sign their documents, or we were expelled. (Interview #24)

3/3. Chinese clouds watch over monks and believers, denying them religious freedom. Here too, the mountains and river alert us to the eco-logical problems in Tibet. The sun, now high in the sky, is fully aware of the current situation and observes what is going on. *Anonymous Tibetan artist, Switzerland, 2020.*

Tibetans were also subjected to another form of mass violence, namely famine. The presence of the PLA in Tibet was an economic burden for Tibetans. They had to feed Chinese troops and provide land and food for thousands of their grazing animals (SHAKYA 1999:93). Furthermore, in violation of Point 7 of the 17-Point Agreement, monasteries were destroyed, had their food stocks dispossessed and were heavily taxed. Altogether, around 90 per cent of Tibetan monasteries have been either destroyed or damaged since 1954, with greater intensity during the Cultural Revolution. Monasteries were major spiritual and educational centres, and also played an important economic role. They provided loans to farms and small businesses and assisted families in times of hardship. The loss of the support provided by monasteries was not compensated at the time by the Chinese authorities. Consequently, rural Tibetans were exposed to extreme poverty and famine (HEATH 2005:18). The famine caused by the Great Leap Forward (1958–1962) was responsible for the deaths of millions of Tibetan and Chinese people. In Tibet, 5 per cent of the Tibetan population died, compared to 2.7 per cent in the PRC (RUOWANG 1998:71). Several witnesses report that, when hardship hit Tibetans before the occupation, they were usually self-sufficient and "did not die from hunger". Nomads, in particular, considered themselves to have a hard, but peaceful life (Interviews #2, #11, #12, #15). The Tibetan population declined further during the Cultural Revolution. The population of Tibet is reported to have dropped by 10 per cent (MANN 2005:338). The distressing situation in Tibet led the 10th Panchen Lama to write his 70,000 Character Petition, dated 18 May 1962 (TIN 1997), to express his concerns about the Tibetans' welfare. In this report, which was intended for the CCP, the Panchen Lama used appropriate and benevolent language to explain the negative impacts of Chinese policies in Tibet. Nevertheless, it was poorly received by Mao, who deemed it a "poisoned arrow" (TIN 1997:xx). In 1964, the CCP subjected the Panchen Lama to an abusive and humiliating struggle session, or thamzing, for fifty days (TIN 1997:xx). He was subsequently detained for 14 years and endured another, more crowded thamzing in Beijing (TIN 1997:xxi), before his sudden death in Shigatsé in 1989. The two reports by the International Commission of Jurists (ICJ 1959–1960) mention atrocities committed during the occupation, and notably examples of thamzing meant to force entire villages into submission by means of atrocities, such as public executions, crucifixion, dismemberment, vivisection, beheading, burying or scalding alive, and even forcing children to shoot their parents, to name a few.

During the Cultural Revolution, many Tibetans were tortured; people had gone mad, and the world did not intervene. (Interview #22)

The statements of the 1949 CPPCC promoting equal rights and a policy of "ethnic unity, autonomy and religious freedom" (QINGYING 2004:112) left room for interpretations. After Mao's death in 1976, the new leaders blamed the Gang of Four – i.e. Jiang Qing (Mao's last wife), Zhang Chunqiao, Yao Wenyuan and Wang Hongwen – for the atrocities committed in the PRC. A new era seemed to be within reach when Hu Yaobang, General Secretary of the CCP, led a Working Group of the Party Central Committee on Tibet, on 22–31 May 1980. On 29 May, he is said to have "made a very sincere and passionate political speech at a gathering of 5,000 cadres in Lhasa" (YAO 1996:287), regarding the situation of Tibetans and the management of Tibet. He laid out a six-point policy (YAO 1996:287-288) for the implementation of measures adapted to Tibet, and for the relief and empowerment of Tibetans (YAO 1996:287–288). However, his corrective measures were short-lived, and he was removed from his position in 1987.

We feel that our Party has let the Tibetan people down. We feel very bad! The sole purpose of our Communist Party is to work for the happiness of people, to do good things for them. We have worked nearly thirty years, but the life of the Tibetan people has not been notably improved. Hu Yaobang, 29 May 1980, Lhasa (YAO 1996:288)

Following softer, more liberal policies in Tibet, Tibetan culture was treated with more indulgence and religious freedom increased. Tibetans rebuilt some monasteries, with or without the support of Chinese authorities, and the number of nuns and monks significantly increased. Many Tibetans committed themselves to reviving their culture, or "at least what was left of it" (Interview #23), such that, by 1986, monasticism and Tibetan cultural traditions had partially recovered. However, the CCP continued to flout the 17-Point Agreement, notably refusing to grant the TAR genuine autonomy. The unhappiness, frustrations and distrust of Tibetans towards Chinese rule persisted and remained unaddressed by the authorities, resulting in the resumption of arrests and executions of political activists in the early years of the 1980s. In his efforts to find a peaceful resolution to the situation in Tibet, the Dalai Lama exposed his Five-Point Peace Plan in 1987 (Chapter 5.2). The CCP responded to the call for dialogue with a propaganda campaign against the Dalai Lama, thus failing to address Tibetans' struggle without resorting to hurtful and violent measures. The Party's reaction triggered the first in a series of peaceful protests in Lhasa, initiated by monks from Drepung monastery on 27 September. On 1 October, a demonstration turned into a riot in response to the public beating of monks by police officers (AI 1988:188). Protesters were arrested and taken to a police station. Tibetans' calls for their release led to further confrontation. According to eyewitnesses, police officers opened fire on the protestors, killing several Tibetans, including children and monks (AI 1988:188). In their statement, however, the Chinese authorities claimed that rioters had seized police weapons and shot their fellow protesters (AI 1988:188). On 5 March 1988, three days of turmoil began in Lhasa. Deadly clashes between Tibetans and police officers disrupted the Mönlam, or the Great Prayer Festival. The violence was exacerbated when 11 monks, including a 13-year-old, were beaten to death in Jokhang temple by police officers (AI 1989:183). In June 1988, less than a year after presenting his five-point peace plan, the Dalai Lama reiterated his appeals for peace and addressed another, more detailed, proposal for reconciliation to the European Parliament in Strasbourg (Chapter 5.2). The CCP rejected dialogue once more, categorically rejecting what it considered to be hostile interference in Chinese internal matters. The Party thus disregarded Tibetans' suffering and responded by not only maintaining, but increasingly reinforcing repression in Tibet. The total number of victims among Tibetans during the events of 1987–1989 is unknown, but could be as high as 400 (DIIR 2018(2):76). Demonstrations resulting in fatalities continued until martial law was imposed by the PRC in Lhasa and its surroundings (Dagzê and Doilungdêqên districts), starting from midnight on 7 March 1989. Later that year, the Dalai Lama was awarded the Nobel Peace Prize for his advocacy for peace and a non-violent approach to the issue of Tibet.

Martial law was lifted on 1 May 1990, but a major military presence has been maintained ever since. Over the years, the surveillance of Tibetans has been reinforced, and the Chinese authorities have started arbitrarily and even unlawfully interfering in private matters. The so-called Strike Hard anti-crime campaigns were launched in 1996, targeting suspected or perceived dissidents and religious groups in Tibet. Amnesty International reports that the crackdown "was marked by mass summary trials and executions on a scale unprecedented since 1983." (AI 1997:118). In the same year, the patriotic re-education campaigns were systematised – and subsequently reinforced in 2006 – with increased censorship and accusations against the Dalai Lama. After 2008, the CCP increasingly insisted on designating the Dalai Lama, the CTA and "foreign forces" as the indisputable roots of all of Tibet's ills. Yet, the 2008 Summer Olympic Games in Beijing brought to light the human rights violations in Tibet being perpetrated by the PRC. Starting on 10 March 2008 in Lhasa, the Tibetan uprisings were an urgent appeal to the world concerning the persecution Tibetans had been enduring for decades. At the time, Chinese authorities detained over 1,000 dissidents and warned lawyers not to defend Tibetan cases (AI 2009:107; Interview #24). The number of fatalities amongst protesters is unknown, but is reported to be over 140, although the PRC itself reported only 18 deaths (US Congress Senate 2008:50; RUWITCH 2008). On 20 October 2008, four Tibetans are reported to have been executed by the Chinese authorities following the spring protest that occurred in the same year (Human Rights House 2009). Despite the tragic consequences of the uprisings, the games carried on with flying colours. Surveillance intensified in Tibet, as did repression against Tibetans. The influx of information is still closely monitored via the mass surveillance of public spaces, as well as police intrusions into private homes and civic institutions, in particular monasteries. Consequently, if the local population still seems happy to see foreigners, they refrain from talking to them (Observations #15), fearing arrest, interrogation and accusations of divulging "state secrets" (Interviews #1, #6, #9, #17, #23). As Golok Jigme explains, "we enjoyed receiving foreign tourists, even if they could not talk our language. We always hoped that they would be bringing photographs of the Dalai Lama [which are forbidden] with them." (Interview #23). Western interviewees testify to having been photographed and stalked in Tibet. One of them explains that police officers even took photographs of every page of the personal diary they were carrying (Interview #6). All of the Western interviewees confessed to being concerned that their monitoring might endanger the Tibetans they came across and avoided interacting with them as a result.

In 2008, in my hometown Tukon, 16% of the population was killed for rising up, for peaceful protest. They were both monks and lay Tibetans. People were targeted, not so much our culture. The Chinese closed our monastery. (Interview #7)

The bus I was in suddenly stopped. I saw smoke outside and everyone was running away from it. The situation was agitated between demonstrators and police officers. Shops and cars were burnt. For a week, I was confined in my flat. I wasn't allowed to go out at all. Then, I was authorised to shop for food, but not for more than an hour. After 2008, many Tibetans left Lhasa. Most buildings were destroyed by the authorities and life left the streets. After the protests, we could read slogans such as "Tibetans used the mask of compassion, and now they show their real colours" or "The Army loves its people as deep as the ocean" and "We have to send all our best students to the Army", throughout Lhasa. Lhasa, 10 March 2008 (Interview #17)

Three of my friends were jailed in 2008 after a peaceful protest: Tsering Drakpa, Rinchen Phuntsok and Choegen Gyantse, who eventually disappeared. We don't know if he's alive. I want people to know their names, maybe it will help. (Anonymous source)

I was followed at least twice by policemen in Lhasa. At some point, I was approached by a Tibetan who greeted me and asked me where I was from. I barely had a chance to answer before a man, dressed in a black suit and white shirt, appeared from a side street and stood right next to me for a pretty long time. Without saying a word, he started following me as I was walking away and watched what I was taking photos of. My Tibetan interlocutor left as soon as he saw him. (Interview #16)

2008 Tibetan uprisings. Beijing Road. Stones were employed to combat the lethal weaponry used by the Chinese security forces. *Anonymous photographer, Lhasa, TAR, 2008.*

2008 Tibetan uprisings. Beijing Road. Burned buildings. *Anonymous photographer, Lhasa, TAR, 2008*

2008 Tibetan uprisings. Beijing Road. Burned out Bank of China branch. *Anonymous photographer, Lhasa, TAR, 2008.*

Beijing Road]. Military presence on Lhasa's streets. *Anonymous photographer, Lhasa, TAR, 2008.*

2008 Tibetan uprisings. Potala Palace behind the smoke of tear gas or controlled fires. *Anonymous photographer, Lhasa, TAR, 2008.*

Following the 2008 uprising, posters depicting Tibetans as rebellious and violent incited mistrust and justified the brutal handling of protesters. This poster reminds Tibetans that any criminal act will be very severely punished. *Anonymous source, Lhasa, TAR, 2008.*

Chinese troops on the streets of Labrang. *Anonymous photographer, Amdo, 2008.*

2.2 Tibetans Living in Fear

Their [i.e. activists'] hope is to live in peace and to be free to live their faith without violence. It is not a lot to ask for. Many told me about torture in prisons, often resulting in death. It was nearly on a daily basis. I even personally knew someone wseho was killed in prison by the Chinese. (Interview #6)

Policemen came to my house at night to check everything. They were looking for photos of the Dalai Lama or any other object relating to him. At night-time, we Tibetans are not safe. We are unhappy and, in our head, it is very heavy because we must be careful all the time. (Interview #9)

For Tibetans advocating for the protection of their cultural identity, the repression is systematic. Their every word and deed to protect our culture is seen as political by the Chinese authorities and interpreted as an anti-government threat. (Interview #23)

Testimonies describe a climate of fear, a silent, suffocating violence, felt by Tibetans and foreigners alike. Yet, Tibetans also show their ability to resist terror and to address the repression with restraint, refraining from violent actions that would aggravate the situation. Nonetheless, despite their efforts and persistence, the testimonies related in this study show that even peaceful protests can be brutally dealt with. The CCP considers independent voices and dissidents as enemies of the PRC's national unity and security, punishing them for what it sees as betrayal. Tibetan witnesses say they had no peace of mind when living in Tibet. Police forces are reported to enter and search homes and to carry out arrests mainly at night (Interviews #9, #12, #19). The testimonies also reveal the incomprehension of Tibetans in the face of such violence. One interviewee recalls the story of a friend who was tortured and died from his injuries in prison: "it's frustrating because all Tibetans want is to live in peace with religious freedom. It's not a lot to ask for." (Interview #18). A former nun was jailed and tortured for shouting "Long live the Dalai Lama!" and "Freedom for Tibet!" during a peaceful protest (Interview #24). Arrested and accused of *splitism* or separatism, she was initially sentenced to 9 years of imprisonment, a sentence that was increased to 17 years after she was caught chanting in jail (Chapter 3.1). This is a harsh punishment for merely chanting slogans, as she explains: "I only wished long life to someone. Where's the harm? It wasn't dangerous!" (Interview #24). If the awarding of the 2008 Olympic Games to Beijing drew international attention to the PRC, it had very little impact on the CCP's promotion of and respect for human rights in the country. The Party's priority was, first and foremost, to present the PRC as an exemplary nation and to censor any elements that were considered detrimental to this image. Consequently, the slightest whisper from Tibet was silenced, further isolating the population. Tibetans were left powerless and highly vulnerable to abusive and prejudiced treatment. In the documentary *Leaving Fear Behind* (2008), the Tibetan filmmaker

Dhondup Wangchen, in collaboration with Golok Jigme, defied censorship and gave a voice to 108 Tibetans from remote areas in Eastern Tibet, between October 2007 and March 2008. The testimonies illustrate the exclusion of Tibetans from the games, whereas citizens from all across the world were eagerly waiting to attend Beijing's celebrations. The Tibetan interviewees explain that the event gave them no reason to rejoice. They lacked freedom, their poverty had worsened, as prices rose due to the games, and the absence of the Dalai Lama aggravated their moral distress. In March 2008, in Beijing, their voices were heard. The documentary was released, revealing to the world the ongoing human rights violations in Tibet and the suffering inflicted on Tibetans. The reaction of the CCP was swift. Dhondup Wangchen and Golok Jigme were arrested and sentenced to prison, for 6 years and 7 months respectively. Golok Jigme was sent to Kachu prison, where he was tortured for 52 days (KOLLER 2015).

Several detention facilities were mentioned by interviewees, including re-education through labour camps, where they or Tibetans they knew were imprisoned (Kachu, Chushul, Deyang and Mianyang Prisons). Two were reported to be particularly notorious for torturing political prisoners, namely Drapchi prison and the Gutsa, both located in Lhasa. Arrests and enforced disappearances often occur at night, without any warning. A witness also talks about "secret flats within Lhasa where Tibetans are tortured" (Interview #16). According to Golok Jigme, the witness may be referring to the numerous small, inconspicuous police stations scattered throughout the capital (Interview #23). They may be what are known as "secret black jails" (HRW 2009) in the PRC – that is, secret detention facilities that attract no attention from the outside and that are used for abusing detainees. Many prisoners never reach a courtroom, and lawyers rarely risk defending Tibetans (Interview #24). They seldom have access to a lawyer or defence counsel. They are not informed of their rights and are denied bail (USDOS 2021). Witnesses state that the arbitrary jail sentences are influenced by various fluctuating factors, such as the prisoner's prior convictions, compliance with the authorities and perceived dissidence, with some detainees being handled more severely than others. Sentences may also be alleviated thanks to the intervention of the international community. These different elements also determine the treatment of prisoners (Interviews #18, #23, #24), i.e. their exposure to physical and psychological torture, such as beatings, humiliation, exhausting forced labour, sleep deprivation, solitary confinement and lack of access to edible food and potable water, to name a few (Interviews #9, #10, #23, #24). However, the most painful experience for the witnesses interviewed was to be forced to accuse the Dalai Lama of all the evils of the Tibetans, whether in prison or during a patriotic re-education session (Chapter 4.3). Golok Jigme explains that prison guards in Tibet, when they have recourse to torture or ill-treatment of any kind, try to ensure that detainees do not die in custody, but shortly after their release, in an attempt to pin the blame on external causes. Thus, torture victims may be freed before the end of their sentence, when their health has dangerously declined due to mistreatment (Interview #23). Moreover, the USDOS states that "[r]eports from released prisoners indicated some were permanently disabled or in extremely poor health because of the harsh treatment they endured in prison." (USDOS 2021). Other witnesses state that if they die in jail, their bodies are not handed over to their families, but burnt without notice "to hide their wounds, the proofs of their torture" and to deny the victim's right to a funeral according to the Buddhist tradition (Interviews #1, #21). One witness admits that she is still afraid of police officers here in Europe, as a result of the mistreatment she, and her family, endured in Tibet:

> *If the police wants to beat someone up, they don't need a reason. My family and I were assaulted in our own house. I was 7 or 9 years old. The police arrived, and my sister, who was in her early twenties, was violently slapped, just for turning her*

head away from them. It was so violent; she had the mark of the hand on her face. We don't have rights; we are beaten and tortured for no reason and at any age.(Interview #10)

A few days after our peaceful protest in 2008, things changed. Tibetans got arrested in their own home, at night-time. With no trial, court or lawyer, they faced 3 to 12 years in prison. There is no way to know where they were taken to and if they would be back. (Interview #12)

When I was arrested for peacefully demonstrating for the return of the Dalai Lama and for the freedom of Tibet, I was first taken to the Gutsa Prison. With another nun, we were sent to a so-called court. I was sentenced to 9 years in prison and she was sentenced to 8 years. Then I was transferred to Drapchi, a prison that's very feared by political prisoners. In prison, one of my punishments was forced labour. The tasks were very hard and dirty. I had to plant vegetables and for fertilizer, I had to empty the toilets and septic tanks. There was also intense indoctrination. (Interview #24)

Besides the humiliating physical harm, such as the slap received by this young Tibetan woman (Interview #10), or the gruelling tasks carried out in a filthy environment described by our witness (Interview #24), such behaviour from Chinese official representatives sends a message to Tibetans: they consider and treat them as inferior beings, who owe them, and thus the CCP, complete submission. The relatives of convicted dissidents are also the object of suspicion and closely monitored. The pressure hanging over them was expressed by a witness, whose father had been arrested for participating in a peaceful protest and died in prison. Aggravating her grief, she had to live with the constant dread of being spied on. She feared being accused of a crime she did not commit and then being punished for it. For the CCP, she was a prime suspect of "terrorist activities" and was forced to flee Tibet with her husband (Interview #11). In Lhasa, Jokhang Temple and its kora are a good example of the visual violence exerted on Tibetans. Acts of intimidation are visible at the holy site, which is sealed off by secured entrances and exits. Armed, soldiers in combat gear are posted all around the kora, in the streets and on rooftops, and regularly patrol among the pilgrims. Fire extinguishers and the metallic snare poles soldiers carry can be seen in other sensitive places, such as at the Tibetan border (Observations #15). These are dark reminders of the self-immolation of 157 Tibetans (Chapter 5). This intimidating visual violence is exacerbated by what seems to be a military station close to Jokhang Temple, from where one can hear, and sneak a peek at, soldiers shouting and conducting noisy military training exercises, in total contrast with the pilgrims' peaceful singing of mantras (Observations #15). Moreover, in addition to the pervasive military presence, pilgrims and travellers are further surveilled by police officers, undercover government employees (Interview #16) and countless cameras. One observer offered a more nuanced opinion, claiming that "the obvious presence of the army and police is part of some show that China wants us to see, to pretend everything in Tibet is under control." (Interview #6).

Barkor, in front of Jokhang Temple. We can see that, in 2003, there was no secured entrance and no significant military presence at the site. The Tibetan market pictured here has been replaced by numerous tourist shops all around the kora. *Anonymous photographer, Lhasa, TAR, 2003*

Barkor, in front of Jokhang Temple. Armed soldiers facing Jokhang Temple.
Anonymous photographer, Lhasa, TAR, between 2015 and 2020.

Barkor. Soldiers doing their rounds at Jokhang Temple. They are carrying a snare pole to immobilise suspects, or in the most extreme cases, self-immolating Tibetans. They also seem to be carrying what may be tarps, which certainly serve in this case to hide a self-immolation from public view.

Anonymous photographer, Lhasa, TAR, between 2015 and 2020.

Barkor. Soldiers doing their rounds at Jokhang Temple with similar equipment. Notice the small white marquee on the rooftop in the background. *Anonymous photographer, Lhasa, TAR, between 2015 and 2020.*

Barkor. Soldiers and police officers are posted all around the kora, in the streets and in white marquees on rooftops. *Anonymous photographer, Lhasa, TAR, between 2015 and 2020.*

Barkor. On the left, two soldiers are posted at the entrance of what seems to be a military station. *Anonymous photographer, Lhasa, TAR, between 2015 and 2020.*

Barkor. Soldiers with fire extinguishers. Another dark reminder of the self-immolation of 157 Tibetans. *Anonymous photographer, Lhasa, TAR, between 2015 and 2020.*

Barkor. Armed soldiers and police officers at one of the secured entrances to the Jokhang Temple site. *Anonymous photographer, Barkor, TAR, between 2015 and 2020.*

We used to celebrate Losar and other Buddhist festivals in Lhasa. But there were so many fully armed police officers, it brought tension and fear. It was very difficult to pray and meditate, because officers surrounded us and we were scared. (Interview #10)

The establishment of the Tibet Autonomous Region in 1965, may have been inspired by a somewhat colonial *divide et impera* strategy. With secured borders now separating Tibetans, travelling in and out of the TAR is extremely difficult, if not impossible, for Tibetans. The significant presence of Chinese workers throughout the TAR and the development of mass tourism – 40 million tourists in 2019 according to Xinhua News Agency (XINHUA 2020) – suggest that Han Chinese enjoy considerably more freedom to travel than Tibetans. Indeed, the vast majority of tourists come from the PRC. Foreigners, who are subject to constantly changing travel constraints, restrictions or even bans, are far from representing the bulk of visitors to this region (Observations

#15; Amnesty International 2021). Tibetans wanting to travel to Lhasa from Amdo or Khan need to obtain two documents: a Chinese ID card and a special permit (or tong xin certificate). Tibetans can obtain a Chinese ID card from the age of 18, but according to testimonies, about 80 per cent of them would not be granted a passport enabling them to leave the country (Interviews #15, #16, #18; Freedom House 2021). According to this witness, the CCP does not grant visas and travel permits to Tibetans out of fear that they would go to India to see the Dalai Lama and to talk to exiles (Interview #3). This witness also explains that travelling is further impeded by the inconsistent restrictions that the CCP imposes on Tibetans, preventing them from attending lectures by Buddhist monks and participating in pilgrimages and celebrations, even within the Tibetan territories. For instance, the CTA claims that, in January 2017, the CCP imposed strict travel restrictions on Tibetans seeking to participate in the 34th Kalachakra Initiation, led by the Dalai Lama in Bodh Gaya, India. Even after obtaining their (expensive) legal travel documents, the Tibetans were forced to return home. They were told by the Chinese authorities that, in the interim, the event had been designated as criminal (DIIR 2018/1:12–13; USDOS 2018). These few examples corroborate the statements made by Tibetans regarding their unequal treatment when it comes to freedom of movement, as compared with Han Chinese citizens (Interviews #2, #3, #10, #18, #21). Today, these strict policies force many Tibetans seeking to flee from the PRC to take significant risks, often by crossing the Himalayas on foot or by attempting to reach a neighbouring country hidden in lorries, both of which are harsh and life-threatening endeavours. As one escapee relates: "We hid in boxes in a lorry. We knew we had one in two chances to survive or to die of suffocation, but we had no choice" (Anonymous source 2019). Over the years, the PRC has increased pressure on anyone involved with Tibetan issues, transcending borders in an attempt to impose its rule and to prevent asylum seekers from succeeding.

2.3 Atrocity Crimes in Tibet

In 1944, Lemkin published his Axis Rule in Occupied Europe: Laws of Occupation, Analysis of Governance, Proposals for Redress, in which he introduces the term "genocide" (LEMKIN 1944:79), combining the words "genos" (tribe) and "cide" (killing). Lemkin had a far-reaching vision and identified the various components of genocides, as acts aiming to eliminate the targeted population's actual existence. His conception of genocide does not always entail the immediate destruction of a nation and its people. It should rather be seen as a process, a coordinated, two-step plan of action, aiming first to eradicate the national patterns of the oppressed group and then to forcibly assimilate this group, by imposing the national patterns of the perpetrator (LEMKIN 1944:79). In that respect, the aim of genocide is the "disintegration of the political and social institutions, of culture, language, national feelings, religion, and the economic existence of national groups, and the destruction of the personal security, liberty, health, dignity, and even the lives of the individuals belonging to such group" (LEMKIN 1944:79). He further indicates that genocide "is directed against the national group as an entity, and the actions involved are directed against individuals" (LEMKIN 1944:79). These actions can occur in times of war or peace (LEMKIN 1944:93). Genocides have been recognised worldwide, resulting in the 1948 United Nation Convention on the Prevention and Punishment of the Crime of Genocide. However, the convention's text focuses on mass extermination on the biological level, overlooking the complexity of Lemkin's concept of genocide, and notably the central cultural component of such violence.

> *Art. II.* In the present Convention, genocide means any of the following acts committed with intent to destroy, in whole or in part, a national, ethnical, racial or religious group, as such:
>
> (a) Killing members of the group;
> (b) Causing serious bodily or mental harm to members of the group;
> (c) Deliberately inflicting on the group conditions of life calculated to bring   about its physical destruction in whole or in part;
> (d) Imposing measures intended to prevent births within the group;
> (e) Forcibly transferring children of the group to another group. (1948 UN Convention on the Prevention and Punishment of the Crime of Genocide)

The United Nations has recognised four genocides: against the Armenians (1915–1916), against the Jews and Roma (1939–1942), against the Tutsi (1994) and against the Bosnians (1995). Nevertheless, the issue of genocide can still lead to controversy and tensions between states. For instance, Turkey refuses to recognise the Armenian genocide, while other confirmed cases of genocidal acts have been given no official status as full genocides, as in the case of Tibet, where the Legal Inquiry Committee reported in 1960 that acts of genocide were being perpetrated (LIC 1960:17). Numerous facts and observations reported in this study tend to corroborate the claim that the violence in Tibet meets the criteria for genocide laid down in the article cited above, namely insofar as it involves the intention to destroy, in whole or in part, the Tibetan peoples. The repression, persecution and killing in Tibet has targeted individuals on the basis of their membership in a specific group, particularly the Buddhist community, which represents the majority of Tibetans regardless of their social status. The 1959 uprising resulted in a mass atrocity, followed by decades of further unnatural deaths. The policies and measures undertaken by the CCP show a pattern of repeated destructive actions which deliberately inflict adversity on Tibetans. They involve numerous forms of physical and psychological brutality, such as enforced disappearances, extensive surveillance systems to monitor the population, arbitrary detentions, patriotic re-education campaigns, disruptions of Tibetans' social and cultural ties, and the imposition of obstacles to their spiritual fulfilment. Some groups are targeted more intensively, notably nuns, monks and nomads, whose precarious living conditions and the hardship they undergo threaten their way of life, their economic survival and their well-being. Although a Tibetan genocide has not been legally recognised, crimes against humanity, involving "acts that are part of a widespread or systematic attack directed against any civilian population" (UN 2014:1), have certainly been committed. Moreover, Lemkin's conception of genocide makes possible a more in-depth understanding of the scope of violence in Tibet. The summary of the events given above highlights the intransigence of the CCP in its treatment of Tibetans. The PLA takeover and the Chinese occupation of Tibet are portrayed as a liberating and civilising mission, thus implying that Tibetans are inferior to Han Chinese. By promoting the supposedly peaceful approach of the PLA, the CCP claims to have obtained the Tibetans' approval of the Chinese intervention in Tibet and, therefore, of its status as part of the PRC. As "second-class" citizens, Tibetans are forced to submit to Chinese rule, even when the latter causes suffering. The PLA crushed revolts and persecuted the population in order to discourage any signs of dissidence, thus further inflaming the conflict by resorting to violence. The CCP's lack of consideration for the population was also marked by the 17-Point Agreement, which was the product of forced cooperation and which was recklessly implemented by the Party. Taking no account of local specifics, the CCP hastened reforms and looted monasteries, subjecting Tibetans to extreme poverty and starvation. Lemkin considers that actions endangering peoples' health should be counted among the biological and physical techniques of genocide, as they lead to the decline of the oppressed population without the use of executions. These techniques notably include depriving victims of necessities, such as sufficient food, appropriate clothing, warm and sanitary housing, and medication (LEMKIN 1944:86–90). He further explains that mass killings are used against leaders and intellectuals, who are considered national icons and suspected of leading resistance, as well as ordinary members of the targeted population (LEMKIN 1944:88–89).

Lemkin thought beyond the biological extermination of targeted groups. His study on the violence suffered by non-Germanic populations before and during World War II allowed him to identify eight spheres in which genocides could be committed, namely the political, social, cultural, economic, biological, physical, religious and moral (LEMKIN 1944:82–90). As Lemkin writes, "The enemy nation within the control of Germany must be destroyed, disintegrated, or weakened in different degrees for decades to come." (LEMKIN 1944:81). Lemkin gives examples of what he called the "techniques of genocide" in the various fields mentioned above. Similar forms of abuses in Tibet were identified during interviews and will be related in the following chapters, with a focus on culture-based violence. In-depth studies in all areas of society are essential for understanding, identifying and recognising such techniques – that is, for establishing what constitutes genocidal aggression or potential triggers of violence, knowledge which would help to prevent future mass atrocities, as it could be applied to other situations of violence against endangered peoples. In Tibet, the cultural, religious and moral spheres have been significantly affected, including violations of the freedom of expression, religion and education. Lemkin's examples of violations of cultural rights by the conquering state include prohibitions on speaking one's native language (LEMKIN 1944:84), the dispatching of the state's own teachers to the subjugated region to instil its cultural principles (LEMKIN 1944:84 - Art. 4, Art. 6c. and 6d), the destruction of cultural heritage and the imposition of restrictions on artists and intellectuals (LEMKIN 1944:84). Religious and moral violations, for their part, entail an attempt to interfere in the faith and values of subjugated peoples (LEMKIN 1944:90). Lemkin described the techniques of genocide as a "concentrated and coordinated attack upon all elements of nationhood" (LEMKIN 1944:82). From the beginning of the occupation, the CCP's assaults were directed against those things that made Tibet a nation, seeking to eradicate its political and societal organisation through a long process consisting of a series of coordinated actions. The methods employed also entailed exclusionary, segregationist and discriminatory practices against Tibetans, resulting in inequitable opportunities in education and employment, as well as placing Tibetans in a situation of enhanced economic vulnerability. Several witnesses underlined that the physical and psychological violence perpetrated against Tibetans who try to preserve their way of life, values and identity, is on the increase, as a result of both the 2008 uprisings and Xi Jinping's accession to power in 2013 (Interviews #1, #6, #7, #8. #11, #12, #18, #22). The Party continues to fail to protect all its citizens, i.e. by preserving their human security. Tibetans are entitled to live without fear of physical brutality and to be provided with adequate food and economic relief. They ought to be protected against indignity and to enjoy equal rights with Han Chinese (CDA 2015:9). Tibetans have the right to the highest attainable standard of physical and mental health, which the Chinese authorities have failed to provide, even though physical and mental well-being is crucial for their survival and pursuit of happiness. The freedom to access knowledge and to be creative, belonging and enjoying self-fulfilment all presuppose the respect of cultural rights. However, since Tibetans have little opportunity to decide for themselves, they struggle to meet the basic needs necessary to their welfare.

> *I believe that when China invaded Tibet, they wanted to get rid of Tibetans. As they can't kill everyone, I think because of the international pressure, they persecute Tibetans differently and hide everything, silence everyone.* (Interview #2)

> *We may not use the same words as you, but we understand that genocides happen when a nation wants to eliminate another one, from the people to their cultural heritage.* (Interview #4)

> *When I lived in Tibet, I knew about genocide. I believe it's what has been happening, from my experience and from what I heard from older people.* (Interview #7)

> *The violence has become systematic. After 1987, the reprisals against Tibetans were already severe, but they weren't as brutal as today.* (Interview #22)

> *I think from the very beginning, the Chinese authorities wanted to eradicate Tibetans and their culture. They first used weapons and, as they became a strong political and economic power, they progressively bought the silence of states and partners. China pretends to be an exemplary and modern nation. In reality, Chinese laws were made to protect the Party, not the citizens. With its involvement in human rights, as in the UN, China seeks to reinforce its image among the international community, but in reality human rights in China merely exist on paper. I was jailed three times and when I was mentioning laws and human rights to the prison guards, they never responded.* (Interview #23)

Conclusion

Several interviewees expressed the feeling of having been dehumanised and forced to live in an open-air prison in Tibet. The PRC interprets Tibetans' social malaise as a threat to its authority and to the unity of the country. It represses, rather than addresses, grievances, and its position does not seem to be negotiable. Consequently, for the PRC, the security of the state, and of the powers that be, has priority over the security of the population. In Tibet, this entails a more severe approach to social order based on security directed against perceived enemies, through the use of intelligence, widespread restrictions on freedoms, a large military and police presence, and restrictive law enforcement limiting religious activities and other means of expression. Such an approach cannot bring sustainable peace, as it does not address insecurities and long-standing inequalities, but rather reinforces perceived threats on both sides (HAMBURG 2021:103).

Tibetan witnesses expressed their incomprehension at the human rights violations they face in their daily lives, restricting their freedoms and endangering them and their loved ones. Even if a full genocide against Tibetans has not been legally recognised, crimes against humanity have clearly been committed in Tibet. Recently, there have also been several accusations that the TAR was the testing ground for many of the genocidal techniques being used today against the Uyghurs in Xinjiang, as well as members of other Muslim minorities (HRW 2018 / United States Senate Committee on Foreign Relations 2018). As Charny states, "[g]enocides are most apt to occur in states ruled by totalitarian governments [...]. The territorial expansion provides incentives to states to destroy indigenous peoples directly and indirectly, by malign neglect of their needs, making them vulnerable to poverty, isolation, impeding well-being, powerlessness" (CHARNY 1999:496). While it is not possible to know with certainty what the Chinese government's long-term goal is in Tibet, its actions continue to threaten the lives of Tibetans and lead to the disappearance of their authentic and ancestral cultural identities and references. The notion of cultural genocide was, however, not used here due to its ambiguity. The risk is that, in addressing cultural genocide, we separate out Tibetans' cultural existence and their biological survival, when in reality both are intertwined.

3

FORCED CULTURAL ASSIMILATION

Cultural rights protect the rights for each person, individually and in community with others, as well as groups of people, to develop and express their humanity, their worldview and the meanings they give to their existence and their development through, inter alia, values, beliefs, convictions, languages, knowledge and the arts, institutions and ways of life. (OHCHR 2010:5–6)

Introduction

The CCP seems unable – or unwilling – to address cultural diversity in the PRC in a constructive and instructive way. Consequently, it resorts to direct or indirect violence in order to impose its idea of "ethnic unity", meaning, inter alia, cultural identities and expressions that only the Party can authorise. Acculturation occurs when continuous and direct contacts between individuals or groups from different cultural backgrounds result in progressive changes in cultural references. Forced cultural assimilation, on the other hand, entails a partial or total enforced rejection of one's culture, to the detriment of the targeted individual or community. Lemkin calls "absorption" an assimilation that has been fully completed (LEMKIN 1944:8). The 2007 Declaration on the Rights of Indigenous Peoples (Art. 8) and the 2007 Fribourg Declaration (Art.

4) reiterate the prohibition on forced assimilation in international law. Acts of mass violence, such as genocide, forcefully interrupt the natural process of cultural change. In his 70,000 Character Petition, the 10th Panchen Lama expressed his concerns about the CCP's concept of modernisation and improvement in Tibet, which focuses on economic development to the detriment of Tibetans' identity and way of life. He warns that once a society's cultural landmarks, such as its language, dress and customs, have disappeared, the society itself will vanish (TIN 1997:69–70). This chapter will focus specifically on the violations of cultural rights committed in Tibet, as the PRC carries out the forced cultural assimilation of the territory. The testimonies cited in this chapter will also reveal interviewees' dismay at being trapped in an endless conflict not of their own making. They also underline that under the assaults against Tibetans' way of life and cultural identity lies a preponderant economic interest. Several methods of repression used by the Chinese authorities reported in this chapter are referred to by Lemkin as techniques of genocide (LEMKIN 1944:82–90). As stated in Chapter 1, four main topics were identified as salient during the interviews: monastic life, education, language, and nomads and the environment. Most of the 46 articles of the 2007 Declaration on the Rights of Indigenous Peoples concern cultural rights. As human rights, these rights are indivisible, interdependent and interrelated. They are equal in importance. However, depending on the issues being discussed, certain specific rights will be more directly affected than others. These are thus indicated at the beginning of each sub-chapter.

Lhasa. Propaganda poster with the slogan "Our mother's name is China", promoting China's ethnic unity and cultural diversity. The young woman on the right is Tibetan and the one on the left is Han Chinese. *Anonymous source, Lhasa, TAR, after 2008.*

3.1 Monasticism

> 2007 Declaration on the Rights of Indigenous Peoples. Article 3, Article 5, Article 11, Article 12, Article 14, Article 20, Article 25, Article 31, Article 33, Article 34

Sera Monastery under military surveillance. *Anonymous photographer, Lhasa, TAR, 2008.*

The centrality of Buddhism in Tibet's economic, social and cultural life has been targeted by the CCP from the very beginning of the occupation, via increasing interference in Buddhist affairs in order to impose its authority and control over Buddhism, which is perceived as a threat to social stability and national unity. Yet, according to Article 18 of the Universal Declaration of Human Rights, signed by the PRC, every individual has the right to enjoy religious freedom without fear of persecution. In Tibet, however, Tibetans are subject to the Chinese interpretation of this right: expressions of their spirituality must be authorised by the Chinese government. Buddhism counts amongst the five official religions recognised by the state, alongside Taoism, Islam, Protestantism and Catholicism. However, this does not mean that believers and practitioners are safe from monitoring, persecution and discrimination (USDOS 12 May 2021). In Tibet, for instance, the authorities have a firm grip on monasteries' activities, teaching and funding, and restrict access to them. Thus, the severe restrictions imposed by state regulations impede the exercise of legitimate religious freedom, which consequently places Buddhism under the control of the Chinese government (USDOS 30 March 2021). The adverse consequences of the lack of religious freedom are particularly felt by nuns and monks in monasteries. The patriotic re-education sessions, evictions and monitoring place them at risk of persecution. The CCP claims that Tibetans belong to the "Motherland" and are de facto Chinese. They only need to be "re-educated". Patriotic re-education aims to impose loyalty to the PRC on Tibetans. Initially directed towards nuns and monks, it is now extended to everyone in Tibet, children as well as adults. Through the discourses of its dutiful government employees, the Party dictates its truth and its understanding of religion, law and history (BARNETT 1999:189).

One interviewee deplores the Party's rules and mandatory thinking imposed on clergy in their monasteries, explaining that its incompatibility with Buddhism puts nuns and monks under tremendous pressure (Interview #22). Moreover, monasteries are forced to display portraits of CCP leaders and Chinese flags (USDOS May 2021). According to witnesses, while the frequency of the patriotic re-education meetings varies from one monastery to the next, they take place regularly and can be as frequent as three or four times a week (Interview #22). Chinese governmental representatives frequently interrupt nuns and monks during their prayer and meditation sessions for inspections and patriotic re-education routines. The witnesses confess that the patriotic re-education sessions caused them and their fellow monks a great deal of suffering. They were constrained to reject their faith, knowledge and values, and – even more painfully – they were forced to openly disavow the Dalai Lama. In his monastery, this witness explains monks were forced to agree with the statement that "if there is violence in Tibet, it's all the Dalai Lama's fault. The Party cannot be questioned." (Interview #22). Several witnesses confessed that it was the most difficult experience they had to endure, causing a deep moral conflict that even led some nuns and monks to contemplate suicide (Interviews #14, #20, #22, #24; USDOS 2019). They were also forced to recognise the CCP-appointed 11th Panchen Lama, Gyancain Norbu, and to acknowledge that Tibet was part of the PRC. They had to either sign a document containing these statements or give their consent out loud. Thus, they had to reject aspirations of independence and commit to the Chinese government's vision of unity. In order to more easily enforce these statements on nuns and monks, the CCP weakened the traditional and central role of education in monasteries. One witness explains that the CCP hired highly qualified collaborators in various fields, such as Chinese history, law and politics, to "re-educate" monks in his monastery. During the courses, they notably had to read and learn by heart Chinese leaders' speeches and were repeatedly told that "Tibet has been part of China since ancient times". In order to reinforce their indoctrination, the CCP published books and other documents specifically for monasteries (Interview #22).

In *Tibetan Education*, a book bought in Lhasa, Chinese writer Aiming states that the early 20th century saw the decline of Buddhism in Tibet, which he claims resulted from the voluntary renunciation of monasticism by monks (AIMING 2004:23). However, other testimonies stress that the reasons for the decline were reinforced by the destruction of monasteries or the reduced hosting capacity of monasteries that were restored after the Cultural Revolution, as well as by the access restrictions, bans and evictions of nuns and monks. In 2016, the authorities began a campaign to prevent evicted nuns and monks from practising their faith in other monasteries. Ganzi Sertar Larung Gar (built in 1980), one of the world's largest Buddhist institutes, is probably the best-known example of the CCP's desire to control monasticism. The site has been the scene of regular demolitions and evictions of nuns, monks and practitioners over the years (HRW 2014). It is estimated that the Chinese authorities expelled between 6,000 and 17,000 Tibetan and Han Chinese nuns and monks from Larung Gar and Yachen Gar between 2016 and 2019 (USDOS May 2021). The restrictions on entry, temporary stays and residence affect all monasteries. One witness states that in 1948, 600 monks resided in his monastery, but that the CCP lowered this number to 100 monks in the 1980s. The evictions continued, and nowadays only 70 monks are allowed to remain (Interview #14). If access is prohibited to those under 18, this does not mean that older Tibetans can freely embrace monastic life (USDOS 2021). Those Tibetans allowed to be ordained are selected by the Chinese authorities, who also decide the terms and conditions of their spiritual life and assign them to a monastery close to their homes (Interview #14). Thus, nuns or monks may still be forced to return to secular life against their will, taking them away from spiritual fulfilment. One former monk reveals that they all lived in fear of being evicted from the monastery. Young monks under the age of 18 were particularly fearful and would hide in the mountains whenever Chinese government officials came to inspect the monastery and "re-educate" them (Interview #20). The testimonies show how preventing nuns, monks and Tibetans in general from leading a monastic life or making it difficult to fulfil Buddhist spiritual requirements negatively impacts their ability and opportunities to bring meaningful improvements into their community's lives.

> *One of my relatives went to Kham to join a monastery. After 5 years, he was ordered to leave his monastic life and go back home. After that, he wasn't allowed to go anywhere else.* (Interview #19)

> *The Chinese often came to the monastery. Monks may be expelled or allowed to stay for a month or a year. They decide for you. When I was 10, I saw many monks and I had a great interest in them. I was 10 when I join a monastery but was expelled*

when I was 33. I wasn't allowed to stay in a monastery anymore, I couldn't be a monk again. This is my biggest regret, not having been allowed to be a monk for life. As a monk, I was happy, I had peace of mind and compassion. Then I became a layman and sold clothes, food. I had no time for meditation. (Interview #20)

The Chinese intentionally interrupted us when we gathered for our meditation and prayers. They took time on our prayer sessions to educate us. There was no physical violence. The rules on monastic life were strict. They alone could decide if a new nun was allowed to join the monastery. If we didn't follow the rules, we were evicted. (Interview #24)

Monks must adhere to their [Chinese government representatives'] opinions or they are expelled, or even imprisoned. In this case, they are subjected to tough interrogations. The message they send out to monks is that they must love their homeland, China. They also instil that Buddhism is responsible for the problems of China's unity. (Interview #22)

Furthermore, nuns and monks are continuously monitored. An interviewee recalls being followed by officers when he was leaving the monastery. Nowadays, however, he says surveillance staff is increasingly being replaced by cameras, both inside monasteries and in the streets (Interview #9). For his part, another witness explains that Chinese government employees were located in a building close to the monastery, from where they could easily control the monks' comings and goings, as well as conduct surprise inspections of the monastery (Interview #14). Another monk's testimony illustrates the PRC's coercive methods. He explains that, in his small monastery, Chinese representatives selected a leader or gooki amongst the monks to monitor them. Two years later, they elected two more monks. The Chinese officials made frequent visits and held patriotic re-education sessions. Their speeches were translated into the Tibetan language. He stresses that monks were willing to respect Chinese rules and sign the documents they were given, in order to ensure safety and relative peace – not only for themselves and their fellow monks, but also and more importantly for their families. In the event of disobedience, monks could be evicted or jailed. Their relatives could also suffer retaliation, such as losing their employment or livelihood, or being prevented from finding work or pursuing studies (Interview #14). Another monk testifies that Chinese representatives and police officers were deployed inside his monastery or in offices close to it for four to five days once or twice a year. During the patriotic re-education meetings, he recalls that they kept repeating "one country, one religion!". He specifies that what they meant by "country" was, in fact, the PRC. As for "religion", they meant the leaders of the CCP and their ideology. This was all that mattered (Interview #3).

> *We had to obey. We had to express happiness to them, but our heart was hurt. The Chinese sat on chairs in front of us, and the monks are on the floor. They told us 'Don't listen to the Dalai, don't listen to the exiled-government. They don't help you. Listen to us, and you'll be happy.' If we didn't agree, they would close the monastery, and put us in jail. After the conference [the patriotic re-education session], we had to sign a document. One copy for us and the original for the Chinese. To be peaceful, monks in monastery have to respect Chinese laws. If a monk has trouble, it means his relatives will be in trouble too.* (Interview #14)

> *In our monastery, they came once or twice a month to speak about how important the nation was and to remind us who the 'real' Panchen Lama was. They also criticised the Dalai Lama a lot, saying that he was destroying peace in our nation, our family. The Chinese would put the names of all the monks in a bowl and pick 10. These monks had to sign a document stating that the 'Dalai Lama is our enemy' and be photographed with the signed document. For the Chinese, it's supposed to prove that we are no longer devoted to the Dalai Lama. It happened to me. Many monks cried. It's our biggest regret but if we refused, we were expelled. They could even close the monastery.* (Interview #20)

> *What hurts the most is having to hear their accusations against the Dalai Lama, and being forced to endorse, sign, say it out

loud in front of everyone. It is against our conscience. It is an inner conflict that affects us, day and night. For Tibetans who embrace Buddhism, the Dalai Lama is still considered as the Buddha of compassion. Denying him is so painful for nuns and monks, it is such a problem for their conscience, it can drive them to contemplate suicide. But many don't, because it's against Buddhist values. There is no way out, otherwise we are tortured, mistreated, imprisoned. (Interview #22)

I spent 17 years in prison. Forced labour was very hard, but the most painful part was to have been forced to say bad things about the Dalai Lama. In prison, the nuns couldn't endure the indoctrination anymore. I befriended 14 nuns. To bear the pain, we composed songs for the Dalai Lama, songs about freedom and songs denouncing the harsh conditions in prison. We did it in secret, but it was found out. Our sentences were increased from 5 to 9 years. I got 8 more years. (Interview #24)

Many Chinese collaborators are sent to monasteries. With their presence and teachings, they want to prevent monks from protesting. They want to make them obedient. The monks comply to avoid violence and to end the conflict. Peace results in their acceptance that Tibet is part of China and that the Dalai Lama is responsible for their difficulties. This is their strategy: problems always come from outside. (Interview #22)

Nuns and monks have less attachment than lay Tibetans and have a strong Buddhist faith. They can let it go and take responsibility for the consequences of their actions. (Interview #24)

Nuns and monks are particularly vulnerable to persecution not only for their choice of lifestyle, but also for their influence, their knowledge and their early role in non-violent demonstrations. Although most protests are reported to have been peaceful, some turned into riots (Chapter 2) and self-immolations continue to be reported (Chapter 5). Interviewees explain that if they followed nuns and monks in protests or sought answers and instruction from them, this was due the trust they had in them for their education, sincerity, integrity, conscientiousness and ancestral knowledge (Interviews #1, #5, #22, #24). The role of nuns and monks in the intergenerational transmission of information is counteracted by the CCP, as is their involvement in leading protests. Buddhism teaches morality and empathy, encourages self-improvement and puts an equal value on every human being. In their peaceful protests, nuns and monks may be seen as seeking to alleviate Tibetans' suffering and to guarantee them the necessary freedoms to practice the "Dharma" (spiritual practice). Their lesser degree of social and familial attachment may count amongst the main reasons explaining why nuns and monks have been more inclined to protest despite the risks of arrest and persecution (Interviews #1, #5, #22, #24). They also strive to help Tibetans achieve a meaningful existence and reach happiness, notably through spiritual fulfilment. The involvement of monks may be more widespread but according to a former nun, nuns are as involved as monks. If their activities are less well known, this is due to their smaller communities:

> *Large monasteries like Sera or Drepung could welcome up to 10,000 monks. For nunneries, the maximum was 200 nuns, but usually it is 100. In Drapchi prison, we were about 200 imprisoned nuns. In terms of percentage, we are as active as monks.* (Interview #24)

She was arrested during a peaceful protest and served 17 years in prison, during which she was tortured (Chapter 2.1). Two witnesses have relatives who were nuns, and both were jailed for their participation in peaceful protests. One was arrested in 2008 along with all the other nuns in her nunnery (about 70). She was jailed for seven years for asking for the return of the Dalai Lama (Interview #1). In April of an undisclosed year, the other nun was arrested in Barkhor with two of her fellow nuns (Interview #9). They, too, had requested more freedoms and the return of the Dalai Lama. She spent five years in prison in dreadful conditions and was only allowed to have visits once a month. Our witness recalls a devastating experience:

> *It took only a few minutes for the police to arrest her. When I visited my sister in prison, I couldn't recognise her. It was not my sister. She had long hair; they didn't allow her to cut her hair even though she was a nun. She was very pale and thin. They gave her food only once a day. It was pigs' food: all mixed up and with white worms and bugs because it was old and disgusting. She still had to eat it to survive. During the day, the prisoners stayed in jail or were made to stand still all day outside, in the sun, without food or water. They were not allowed to speak or even move. Some regularly fainted. Because of the harsh conditions, many prisoners fell ill like my sister. They are not given any medical treatment. My sister was also beaten by the police in jail with sticks and with electric prods. They even broke her ribs. Many prisoners in Tibet die from starvation, diseases, mistreatment and violent beatings.*
> (Interview #9)

The physical and psychological abuses she had to endure are widespread in prisons in Tibet: inedible food and non-potable water, as well as deprivation, inadequate sanitation, denial of medical care, prolonged exposure to heat or cold, exhaustion, beatings, electroshocks and solitary confinement. Obliging a nun to grow out her hair is a form of violence, since it amounts to denying her identity and faith, and thus her dignity. After her release, she and her family were closely watched and spied on by the police. Our witness recalls: "One night, when we were all asleep, the police arrived and started looking everywhere for photos of the Dalai Lama or anything related to him" (Interview #9). A former monk recounts the peaceful protest in 1996 at Ganden Monastery, which was hosting 900 monks at the time. According to him, between 200 and 300 of the monks were arrested by the police and about 100 disappeared. Many participants were indeed arrested, but no exact number was reported (USDOS 1997). The monastery was shut down for a year, and the monks left, around 500 of them, had to attend intensive patriotic re-education. Monks who resisted and refused to blame the Dalai Lama for "splitism" and "betrayal", like our witness, were definitively expelled from monastic life (Interview #8). Another witness described a peaceful protest that took place in Tehor from 10 to 24 March 2008. About 300 nuns, monks and lay Tibetans gathered to ask for freedom and the Dalai Lama's return. Police officers opened fire on the crowd, killing a 20-year-old monk, whose name was Kunga (HRW 2010):

After the shooting, he was taken back to the monastery by Tibetans, but he died soon after. The police demanded his body or they said they would punish everyone and close the monastery. So, he was taken away to hide what happened. I knew his parents; it was very sad news. When a person dies, we keep the body in our home for prayers, usually for a week depending on the Tibetan calendar. They killed him and didn't respect Tibetan traditions. It was very painful for his family. (Interview #1)

Although Tibetans met the police's demands by handing young Kunga's body over to them, the monastery was still shut down for six months. Strict patriotic re-education and rules were then imposed on the remaining monks. In addition to the killing, police officers further aggravated the suffering of the victim's family by taking his body away from them. They showed disregard for his dignity and prevented his relatives from mourning him according to their beliefs and rituals. A few years later, on 10 March 2012, another monk from the same monastery, called Molan, is reported to have been arrested for possessing and sharing videos of the 2008 protests in Tehor, notably showing self-immolations (Interview #1).

After their release, nuns and monks are often not allowed to return to their monasteries, and the little freedom of movement they had is denied to them. Isolated and closely monitored, they face extreme poverty, enforced idleness and have little prospect of reintegrating into society (Interview #24).

In 2008, I saw leaflets and posters against the wall in my village. Tibet was standing up for human rights and religious freedom. Our demonstrations were peaceful. There weren't many police officers, the village was too small. But 15 minutes away from the village, there was a big monastery, and there were many police officers there. Some officers left the monastery to go to the village. Our Lama made sure the protest would stay quiet and peaceful, so there weren't any arrests that day. (Interview #12)

There is still great poverty in Tibet and Tibetans are on their own. Many monks and nuns who are former political prisoners no longer have relatives when they are released after long prison sentences. They usually don't have access to monasteries anymore. They have no rights, no access to work and are not allowed to receive assistance. They cannot have any contact with anyone, at the risk of serious consequences for them and for those who are associated with former prisoners. It is a strategy to isolate them, reduce them to extreme poverty and thus discourage Tibetans from resisting. (Interview #24)

3.2 Learning Opportunities

2007 Declaration on the Rights of Indigenous Peoples. Article 5, Article 12, Article 13(1), Article 14, Article 15, Article 31.

There are not a lot of schools in villages. Children and their families are transferred to cities. The purpose is economic and to make them learn Chinese. (Interview #1)

The Chinese come every month. They tell us what to do and control what we say. We are told religion is useless and that we have to worship the five Chinese leaders [Mao Zedong, Jiang Zemin, Hu Jintao, Xi Jinping and Deng Xiaoping] we don't even know. (Interview #19)

Education should be an essential ally of freedom and peace, by promoting understanding and fostering communication between peoples and cultures. Hambourg rightly states that education "is a central challenge of our time to provide the foundation for a humane, democratic, and safe course of child and adolescent development, ultimately aiming to protect humanity" (HAMBOURG 2010:13). Education has the power to imbue people with the knowledge and the respect of cultural rights for a peaceful acceptance of other cultural identities (MOREL 2016:3). Article 6 of the Fribourg Declaration recalls that the educational process cannot be limited to initial education, i.e. formal schooling (MEYER-BISCH/BIDAULT 2010:76). Learning throughout life, by having access to a plurality of forms of education, is a right that cannot be restricted. Regardless of their age, gender or origin, individuals should be given the freedom to access extracurricular courses if they wish to do so, to know their rights, to study their language and culture, and to follow religious and moral teachings. In Tibet, this implies Tibetans' right to extend, deepen and share their knowledge, as well as to access a plurality of sources of information, notably in monasteries. In 1960, the LIC recounted the forcible transfers of Tibetan infants and children under the age of 15 from Tibet to the PRC (LIC 1960:51–52). According to the testimonies published, while the Chinese authorities did not systematically justify the removal of Tibetan children from their families, there were found to be two recurrent statements: parents were told to entrust their offspring to the PRC in order both to protect them from starvation and to provide them a better education (LIC 1960:52–58). It was also claimed that children, especially babies, needed to be taken away, as they interfered with their parents' work. Children were promised a better life in the PRC and were allowed to leave Tibet without their parents' consent, which kept them away from their Tibetan roots and education in monasteries. In early letters addressed to their families, however, the children stated that they were doing hard labour, as well as having to learn Mandarin and Communist ideology. After that, their discourse changed radically. The children claimed to be happy and to be receiving an excellent education in the PRC (LIC 1960:54). Overall, the Chinese authorities claimed that the infants and children would return to their families, but the witnesses saw no returns, and neither the children nor their parents protested for fear of reprisals.

Since the mid-1980s, selected Tibetan pupils, essentially from the TAR, have been sent to Chinese boarding schools where they are educated and raised in a Han Chinese environment. These institutions can either exclusively host young Tibetans or they can host a mixture of Tibetan and local Chinese students. In the latter case, however, their education is segregated (POSTIGLIONE/JIAO 2009:898). According to Aiming, in 1984, the second Symposium on Work in Tibet declared that "school education should focus on the Tibetan language" (AIMING 2004:104–105). At the same time, Aiming mentions that, following the Symposium, "1,301 Tibetan primary school graduates, the first group of students from Tibet, were sent to study in 17 high schools in 16 provinces and municipalities" in the PRC (AIMING 2004:105), specifying that the Tibetan pupils were taught Mandarin (AIMING 2004:106). In Tibet, the primary language of education is Mandarin, resulting in the steady decline of the Tibetan language in school curricula (POSTIGLIONE/JIAO 2009:898). Furthermore, boarding schools emphasise political socialisation and ideology (POSTIGLIONE/JIAO 2009:901). Over the years, more Chinese provinces and municipalities have participated in the schooling of Tibetans. By the end of 2005, about 29,000 Tibetan pupils had been sent to the PRC, a number that rose to over 30,000 by 2008, according to official estimates (POSTIGLIONE/JIAO 2009:898). Regarding the teachers, Aiming writes that, as reported by incomplete statistical data, over 20 Chinese provinces and municipalities sent a total of 6,640 teachers to Tibet between the mid-1950s and 1992 (AIMING 2004:110), while Tibetan teachers were trained in Chinese colleges and universities (AIMING 2004:110). The educational quality of this initiative will not be discussed here, but having Tibetan children and teachers educated in the PRC certainly interferes with their cultural identity, especially when it comes to the Tibetan language and contributes to the indoctrination of Tibet. Moreover, as Mandarin has become the prime language of Children's education, their interactions within their families can create painful family situations, as a witness explains:

Children and the youth couldn't speak Tibetan or not well enough, so they weren't able to communicate with their grandparents. The parents also have to learn Chinese to help their children in their studies and homework, as it is not in Tibetan. Between themselves, children speak in Chinese, as they are not allowed to learn Tibetan during their time off. (Interview #18)

In Ngaba (Amdo), schools have closed because of Covid. The teaching staff are working on their reopening and are reorganising the schools' programs. They also take the opportunity to materialise the government's goal to abolish Tibetan lessons. Tibetans are protesting because they fear Covid and school closures will be used as an excuse to further marginalise the Tibetan language in schools and promote China's propaganda. (Interview #23)

My parents didn't want me to go to a Chinese school. They endured the Cultural Revolution and suffered greatly from it. Anything Chinese reminds them of their sufferings and makes them suspicious. Even a newspaper in Chinese hurts them. The vast majority of children around me were in the same situation. For some Tibetans, going to a Chinese school is like going to prison. In my lessons, we talked about their grandparents' story during the Cultural Revolution. At first, children had little, if no interest. Gradually, they began to understand the severity of their elders' experiences. Some even cried because they couldn't understand why China hurt them and why they couldn't keep their culture. The goal of education is to become a good person and not to forget where we come from. (Interview #23)

Education should promote mutual respect and understanding. Yet, the CCP took control of educational institutions and facilities, such as libraries and museums, and is committed to maintain its monopoly on knowledge. The Party's monolithic thinking is secured via the close monitoring of its schools and universities, as well as their respective curriculums. The Party also restricts access to monasteries and traditional high-level spiritual and educational institutions, as well as monitoring their teachings (Interview #23; USDOS 30 March 2021). Students seeking to gain access to higher education must present no risk of dissidence or insubordination, meaning that they must have a good reputation and provide satisfactory references (Interviews #1, #8, #14). One former teacher says that the best Tibetan students are sent to the PRC to study, and often decide to stay there to pursue their higher education. Others leave Tibet after their studies in search of career opportunities in the PRC. Either way, he explains, the migration of promising young Tibetans to the PRC is a loss for Tibet's economy and educational system. While they may come back home, they bring with them "the Chinese language and ideology" (Interview #1). According to the interviewees, although it seems like literacy has improved overall, it has declined in the Tibetan language, suggesting that Mandarin's position in Tibet has been strengthened. Education may be improving in Tibet, but interviewees report that the teaching quality is poor. As discussed above, the transfer of good pupils to the PRC does not help when it comes to raising standards. As Golok Jigme explains, "where I'm from, numerous remote small communities are left behind. Children don't have access to schools." (Interview #23). Another concern comes from Tibet's violent past. Tibetans still bear scars from past atrocities, and numerous Tibetan parents cannot resign themselves to allowing their children to be educated in Chinese schools (Interview #23). The CCP's impunity makes it difficult, if not impossible, for Tibetans to establish a trusting relationship with the Chinese. Golok Jigme addressed the needs of children in remote regions by providing them education that their parents have confidence in. The first aim of the classes was to teach them the Tibetan language. Progressively, he also taught them the recent history of Tibet. After the extensive education they received, some youngsters became teachers of the Tibetan language themselves (Interview #23).

Five Tibetan interviewees educated in Tibet (Interviews #1, #4, #7, #9, #10) explain that they were taught three main subjects in their respective primary schools: Mandarin, the Tibetan language and basic mathematics (taught in Mandarin). Given that Mandarin opens more professional, political and academic opportunities, it is increasingly prioritised over the Tibetan language by young Tibetans. Although a broader range of subjects have become available to them in secondary schools, such as Chinese politics and ideology, the vast majority of these are taught in Mandarin (Interviews #1, #4, #7, #9, #10). Moreover, witnesses deplore the fact that Tibetan issues have been ignored and that Tibet's history has been rewritten, claiming that the material taught does not reflect the reality of Tibetan society. One interviewee even mentions children being punished for asking questions about Tibet's history (Interview #7). Another witness corroborates this testimony: "Young Tibetans want to know the truth about their history and Tibet, but they are afraid to search and ask." (Interview #10). They all felt that the material taught in school was not reliable, and thus considered their parents, grandparents, nuns and monks as the only trustworthy sources of information (Interviews #1, #4, #7, #9, #10, #18). The Party is well aware of the importance of the Dalai Lama in Tibetans' hearts and minds and seeks to replace him with its leaders through patriotic re-education campaigns. Two interlocutors explained that when they were children, they had to sing the Chinese anthem and hoist Chinese flags every morning at school. Pupils also had to wear red scarves, symbolising the CCP (Interviews #1, #7). Children who forgot their scarves were punished. The penalty for a first offense was cleaning chores, while in the case of repeat offenders, corporal punishment was administered, such as being "hit with a stick" (Interview #7). The testimonies also underline the crucial importance of monasteries as educational institutions for both children and adults and as repositories of ancestral artifacts and archives. For Tibetans, they represent one of the last sanctuaries of uncensored information. However, Tibetans under the age of 18, as well as current and former government employees, are banned by Chinese authorities from entering monasteries and receiving instruction (Interview #3; USDOS May 2021). Yet, monasticism provides an education and cultivates values that are cherished in Tibet. Educating children in monasteries is, for Tibetans, essential for ensuring the preservation and transmission of Tibet's heritage to future generations. Consequently, regardless of the prohibitions and risks, the Tibetan interviewees admit that they continued to attend educational events at monasteries, in order to benefit from the monks' knowledge, particularly in Buddhism, the Tibetan language and Tibetan history (Interviews #1, #7).

> *When I was a child, I didn't know there was a struggle between Tibet and China. But I realised we weren't equal, as with the Chinese language we could study, find a job. We had little chance with Tibetan. Also, during primary school, we did not learn anything about Tibetan culture. We had Chinese language, maths and the history of China when it was at war with Japan. We were told we were only one country.* (Interview #10)

> *Patriotic re-education tells us we are the seeds of China, and our nation is China. Our capital city is Beijing. China is like our father and mother and is the best for us. They tell us not to forget our nation and our people, the Chinese people. Tibetan children are our future, but they are being brainwashed by China.* (Interview #1)

> *In Tibet, many young students came to the monastery before their exams to pray and meditate. It helped them, made them more serene and confident for their exams. Unfortunately, today this is no longer allowed.* (Interview #14)

> *Tibetan philosophy is very difficult to learn and to understand. It takes time to study it. Children are sharp and bright; they can learn very quickly. But as they are not allowed to access monasteries to study, it's a way to limit not only the number of monks and nuns amongst adults, but also to lessen Buddhist*

knowledge over time, as their teachings have been drastically shortened and controlled by the CCP. (Interview #20)

Overall, the restructuring of education in Tibet by the PRC has resulted in greater access to schools for children and reduced illiteracy. However, learning opportunities are limited by the CCP's firm grip on information control. The Tibetan interviewees deplore the restrictions on accessing monasteries and intense monitoring of monastic life, denying them freedom of information and the right to religious practice. Elders are an important and trusted source of uncensored information, but with pupils and students studying away from their families and learning Mandarin to the detriment of Tibetan, the intergenerational transmission of knowledge is endangered. In his book, Aiming provides exhaustive figures and statistics, detailing the amounts of money the CCP has spent on the education of Tibetans, as well as the increasing number of primary, secondary schools and universities over the years, with additional data on the growing numbers of pupils and students studying in both Tibet and the PRC. The continuous references to figures may showcase the achievements of the CCP when it comes to educating Tibetans. However, they do not address the deep concerns of Tibetans regarding the decline of their native language in the educational curriculum, the intense patriotic re-education and the censorship of information. As equals to Han Chinese citizens – which is what the CCP claims they are – Tibetans should have access to equal opportunities, notably by being able to study in the Tibetan language without risking discrimination in the employment market in Tibet. The patriotic re-education campaign indicates that the CCP sees education as an effective political medium. Tibetan pupils are sent to the PRC while Chinese teachers move to Tibet, both initiatives contributing to the Tibetan language's decline and the spread of the CCP's one-track thinking and ideology. In such a situation, schools and universities can hardly serve their original purpose of providing uncensored information and knowledge, creating safe and honest debates, and promoting understanding and mutual interest between communities.

3.3 The Tibetan Language

> 2007 Declaration on the Rights of Indigenous Peoples. Article 3, Article 11, Article 13, Article 14, Article 16, Article 31, Article 34.

Language is more than a method of communication between individuals. It is an integral part of our social and cultural life and identity, a means "to conceive, receive and express thoughts, ideas and emotions" (MEYER-BISCH/BIDAULT 2010:66). For all the Tibetan interviewees, the Tibetan language is considered a fundamental component of their cultural identity, a "key driver of a nation" (Interview #23). Their language is also essential for the intergenerational transmission of knowledge (Interview #13). By preserving the Tibetan language, Tibetans ensure that past atrocities suffered by earlier generations do not fall into oblivion. They also protect the ancestral teachings of Tibetan Buddhism (Interviews #7, #22), which are dear not only to Buddhists in Tibet but also throughout the world, including in the PRC. Although Tibetans emphasise the importance of language for preserving cultural survival, few explicitly stress that the Tibetan language is an effective way, through its various forms of expression, to circumvent Chinese censorship. It is reported in Aiming's book that the quote "March towards Tibet, and study the Tibetan language well" (AMING 2004:47) was the official line of the PRC in 1950. The CCP's commitment to and achievements regarding the preservation of the Tibetan language is also repeated several times. The statement made in Point 9 of the 17-Point Agreement, "the spoken and written language and school education of the Tibetan nationality shall be developed step by step in accordance with the actual conditions in Tibet" (Appendix D), may indeed demonstrate the CCP's goodwill but its formulation remains ambiguous enough to give the Party room for flexibility in its application. Consequently, the survival of the Tibetan language quickly became a clear matter of concern for Tibetans. In 1962, the 10th Panchen Lama wrote that he had already noticed a steep decline of the Tibetan language in the social and political spheres and at all levels of the local government, stating that it was progressively becoming a "folk language" (TIN 1997:66).

The danger for an indigenous language is that it is abandoned by the elite, since the middle classes are likely to follow their lead and learn the dominant language to meet the new society's requirements at all levels. A language is further endangered when the younger generations no longer speak or master it. Whether as a consequence of a deliberate choice or not, the abandonment of a language is undoubtedly influenced by the pressures exerted by a state. Instead of improving opportunities for perceived minorities to reduce their vulnerability, restrictive policies lead to the marginalisation of those who do not forfeit their right to speak the language of their choice. Under the occupation, the Tibetan language has increasingly been endangered by Mandarin. The latter became the dominant language in Tibet's economic and political integration. In the 1980s, with the general revival of Tibetan culture, the Tibetan language was given a fresh impetus, but started declining again from the 1990s. Nowadays, Tibetans not proficient in Mandarin face discrimination, marginalisation and poverty. Testimonies that have been collected seem to reveal that the Tibetan language has been effectively relegated to the level of a folkloric dialect, resulting in significant discrimination in employment opportunities. Key positions require fluency in Mandarin, and thus are mostly filled by Han Chinese. Tibetans interested in pursuing a career must demonstrate an excellent command of the new dominant language (Interview #8). For the outsider visiting Tibet – or at least the TAR – it quickly becomes apparent that the vast majority of shops, restaurants and hotels, to name just a few, are run by

Han Chinese (Observations #15). The Tibetan language, by contrast, is associated with limited employment opportunities, less work security and lower status. Migrant Tibetans who move to towns and cities from remote areas of Tibet usually only speak their native language and cluster at the bottom of the labour market, often working on construction sites (Interview #13), notably in Lhasa. Poverty is well hidden, but skeletal frames of street sellers, beggars, farmers and nomads are visible signs of this disparity (Observations #15).

I was a Tibetan language teacher. Because Tibetan is less and less taught in schools, it has become extremely difficult to make a living out of it. (Interview #1)

The hardest thing as an artist in Tibet is to have no right of expression. Our work must be neutral, if we want to be relatively safe and free. If we mention topics like the reality of what's happening in Tibet, history, freedom, the Dalai Lama, we are jailed. (Interview #18)

The CCP's repression of Tibetans who try to promote and develop their language (USDOS 30 March 2021) indicates that the Party is, in reality, unwilling to develop it as promised in Point 9 of the 17-Point Agreement. The CCP strictly controls its use and prevents its development by sanctioning Tibetans who encourage its study and protection. Regarding the persecution of Tibetan language advocates, witnesses mentioned the case of Tashi Wangchuk. In a short New York Times documentary (2015), Wangchuk expressed his view that a "systematic slaughter" of Tibetan culture is underway (KESSEL 2015:2'21'') in Tibet, claiming that the CCP is purposefully impeding the teaching and learning of the Tibetan language. He explained that opportunities to study the Tibetan language have become very limited and recalled that, from primary and middle school through to high school, there is only one Tibetan language course (KESSEL 2015:0'48''). He travelled to Beijing from Amdo, hoping that the media and legal representatives would support his initiative to preserve his people's language. His efforts were in vain. A couple of months later, Wangchuk was arrested at his home in Amdo. Imprisoned for two years, he was allegedly tortured, before being finally condemned to five years in prison for "inciting separatism". Tibetan literary and performing arts, such as opera, are allowed, provided they are cleared from any *backward* features, i.e. anything the CCP considers as contrary to its image and governance (SMITH 2008:48). New songs and dances were introduced, showing the importance of performing arts as a means of propaganda for the PRC (SHAKYA 1999:366–367). The CCP's one-track-thinking policy is very distressing to poets, singers and writers. Although they have the freedom to sing their songs in Tibetan, they cannot express themselves as artists in their own right. The censorship and monitoring of their activities ensure that sensitive topics regarding the Dalai Lama, Tibet's independence, freedom or even Tibetans' unhappiness are nowhere to be found (Interview #18). These artists are restricted to mundane topics, such as love or the beauty of Tibetan nature. This witness further explains that artists often self-censor or when they want to circumvent censorship, they write Tibetan poetry and use symbolism to make it harder for the Chinese authorities to understand. He specifies that most writers were educated in monasteries, and many of them are, or were, monks. This explains their strong command of the Tibetan language. Nevertheless, since they can only express themselves under the cloak of secrecy, their writings can become too complex: "Even Tibetan readers can be discouraged, or they may not understand. It's very upsetting and frustrating." (Interview #18). Thus, the artists who challenge the CCP's authority aloud are considered heroes and highly respected by Tibetans for their courage (Interview #18). In 2020, artists and intellectuals were still being arrested for trying to protect the Tibetan language and culture (USDOS 30 March 2021).

Three Tibetan artists and activists in particular have made a lifelong impression on this witness. The well-known Tibetan singer Gebey is a keen guardian of Tibetan culture. He has spoken out for its preservation, notably with the song "Will Be Perished". Gebey was reported to have been arrested after a concert on 24 May 2014, in Amdo. Our witness states that after his release, he was prohibited from leaving the Amdo area and is currently under constant surveillance (Interview #18). The singer Tenzin Ugyen, the composer of "The Heart's Blood Flows", in which he gives voice to Tibetans' distress, was arrested in 2012 and sentenced to prison. The third artist mentioned is the writer and scholar Tashi Rabten, or *the' u rang* (his pen name). He is reported to have spent four years in prison, after his arrest in 2009 for writing the essay "Written in Blood", discussing Chinese repression. Enforced disappearances and arrests of artists are regularly reported (USDOS 30 March 2021), but reliable details on their fate is lacking due to the opacity of the Chinese legal system and the difficulty of accessing first-hand information from potential witnesses. The testimonies stand in contradiction with the CCP's supposed efforts to preserve the Tibetan language. Regardless of whether or not the ultimate goal of the CCP is to achieve linguistic hegemony in Tibet, through the disappearance of the Tibetan language, the consequences of its policies and repression contribute to its decline.

> *Maybe we can't read, but we can recite poems and sing songs that reflect our feelings and our stories.* (Interview #2)

> *It is especially difficult to live without any freedom of expression. It makes us sad. We have no freedom as Tibetans, not even as artists.* (Interview #18)

> *The goal of the Chinese government is to make the Tibetan language disappear. In the regions of Lhasa and Kham, the level has considerably declined. In Amdo, the language is better protected by strong activism. Young intellectuals know that if our language disappears, so will Tibetans. It creates a lot of anxie-*

ty and encourages them to advocate for it. The government wants the disappearance of the Tibetan language to better control Tibetans, especially activists. The government is very powerful, but so are Tibetans' spirits. We'll see who wins. (Interview #23)

3.4 The Settlement of Nomads and the Environment

2007 Declaration on the Rights of Indigenous Peoples. Article 3, Article 10, Article 20, Articles 25 to 30, Article 32.

I lived high in the mountains. At this time of the year, it's very cold. I had yaks and dris; I was a happy nomad. They were very important for food, clothing and transportation. In my family, we have been nomads for generations. We had good living conditions with the goods we produced. But we have no more freedom, and now I have no authority to live in Tibet as a nomad. I had to sell my animals. It was very upsetting. Nomadic life is as limited as monastic life. (Interview #2)

Both the 2007 Declaration on the Rights of Indigenous peoples and the 2007 Fribourg Declaration emphasise the strong ties between peoples and their lands, which were traditionally owned, occupied, used or acquired. The testimonies underline, even more than their importance as a means of subsistence, the spiritual ties that Tibetans have with their territories and the importance of the preservation of the environment and its biodiversity. A territory is, therefore, the repository of a community's cultural, ecological and economic resources (MEYER-BISCH/ BIDAULT 2010:13). Consequently, the ties between the peoples and their lands ought to be respected and protected. Although the relocation of an individual or a community can bring new opportunities, it can also generate cultural and economic threats to displaced people (MEYER-BISCH/BIDAULT 2010:118). Traditionally, the majority of the Tibetan population was either nomadic or of nomadic descent. Nomadism is considered by the Tibetan interviewees to be an integral part of Tibet's identity. They reckon that it is one of the last and best-preserved repositories of the Tibetan language and culture overall. For their part, former nomads explain that Tibet's wilderness and their herds not only gave them a strong sense of identity and pride, but were also decisive for their survival. As nomads, they were neither rich nor poor, but had decent living standards. More importantly, their nomadic way of life offered them dignity (Interviews #2, #8, #11, #12, #13, #19). Witnesses deplore the rapid decline of the nomadic population, resulting in the progressive disappearance of their traditional knowledge and skills. The PRC's management of the Himalayas and their clearances is an extended project. Cencetti mentions that, over the last 30 years, the most significant shifts that Tibetan nomads have had to face were the fencing policy (1980s) and the grassland division (CENCETTI 2011:47). The interviewees' recurrent grievances focused specifically on the financial burdens imposed on them and their forced settlement in new villages, discussed below, or in cities. According to Chinese authorities, restrictions on nomadism have two primary purposes: 1) the improvement of nomads' living standards, notably by making education and healthcare more accessible; 2) the protection of the natural environment (SULEK 2016:4; Observations #15). Witnesses believe instead that the CCP wants to monitor nomads, just like all other Tibetans, and to impede cultural self-expression. They explain that the Chinese authorities need nomads to be tracked constantly, so that their official representatives can carry out patriotic re-education campaigns. But since nomads follow seasonal flock movements, it is difficult to pinpoint their movements. This is one of the reasons for which the CCP wants to enforce their settlement (Interview #8). A former nomad recalls that in remote regions, Chinese officials would still visit nomadic areas two or three times a month, in search of photographs of the Dalai Lama, the possession of which is punishable by law (USDOS May 2021) They demanded that the nomads raise Chinese flags over their tents and hang pictures of the five Chinese leaders inside. (Interviews #2). Our witness added with a wry smile: "They must be our new gods." (Interview #2). Tibetan interviewees declare that the CCP orders contemptuous "conferences", i.e. patriotic re-education sessions, to discredit the Dalai Lama and the CTA.

> *They try to convince us that the Dalai Lama is against us, doesn't help us and that our country is China.* (Interview #2)

> *We are told that communist leaders are our only gods. We are told to pray them and not Buddha, but in our hearts, we don't. It doesn't make sense.* (Interview #13)

According to testimonies, the Party forces nomads to submit to its authority and renounce nomadism by impoverishing them and imposing precarious living conditions, notably through the implementation of land access restrictions and taxes, as well as limiting livestock and grazing, so as to discourage or even prevent the younger generations from taking over. Former nomads describe different methods that have been used to enforce their settlement. The Chinese authorities can, for instance, progressively limit the quantity of livestock the nomads are allowed to own, until their herd becomes too small to make a living off of (Interview #2). They can also prohibit them, as well as young people from keeping animals (Interview #8). Moreover, they regularly reappraise taxes on the nomads' livestock, increasing them without warning (Interviews #2, #13). Some nomads try to survive by doing extra work for farmers, but their basic income often remains insufficient (Interview #11). They also have to go through patriotic re-education and monitoring. The implementation of stricter policies and the significant financial burdens are, one witness states, a strategy used by the CCP to force nomads to migrate to cities or settle in new villages explicitly built to accommodate them (Interview #19). As a result, former nomads confess that their former lifestyle has progressively slipped out of reach. One witness says his community was first impoverished and then promised more significant income opportunities in towns and cities if they agreed to settle there:

We had to gather to attend a conference [patriotic re-education]. The Chinese talked about the Chinese leaders and incited us to go to cities by offering us money. The amount depended on families and the number of family members. They said we would have an easier life and more money. Some young nomads and families believed them and sold their livestock. Some families receive money to move to cities, but the amount is insufficient and quickly runs out. They are left without financial resources. (Interview #11)

At the very beginning, things were rather peaceful with the Chinese. I was a young nomad; I had to watch the herds non-stop and all alone. It wasn't easy. The Chinese came to us to buy leather, cheese, butter. But as I grew up, we started to have to pay taxes to the Chinese. (Interview #12)

The Chinese government has a lot of money, but Tibetans don't actually get much of it. Tibetans still have to pretend they receive a lot in front of the media, officials and foreigners. (Interview #20)

China pretends everything is fine and that our economy is doing well. Although in Kham nomads are richer than us, as for now, in reality, nomads are generally very poor. (Interview #2)

In early times, nomads were spread out and didn't know each other. They had no address. The police wants to group them and give them names so they can indoctrinate them. Nomads' new houses are like prisons. They are made pretty with flags along the main roads for everyone to see. (Interview #8)

A traditional black nomad's tent, surrounded by livestock. This picture was taken at the Kharola Glacier tourist hotspot, on the way to Shigatse. The discreet presence of these nomads may be fortuitous or calculated, in order to demonstrate the preservation of nomadism in Tibet. *Morel, Kharola Glacier, TAR, 2019.*

Village for settled nomads. *Morel, TAR, 2019.*

The interviewees feel that they were let down and lied to. As one of them expressed it: "China tells us that life is easier in cities, but it's a lie. When we arrive in cities, we can't find a job because we only speak Tibetan." (Interview #2). As discussed in the previous chapter, the language barrier is a problem and a source of discrimination and marginalisation. The employability of nomads is limited in towns and cities, and if they do find work, wages are often hardly sufficient to cover the basic needs given the higher expenses they must meet. Nomads remain in a vulnerable position and the possibilities for improving their situation are very limited. Consequently, some rely on government assistance and on the sale of caterpillar fungus for their subsistence (Interview #19; SOD-NAMKYID/SULEK 2017:145–146), while others are in debt to wealthier individuals in the cities (Interview #11). Along the main tourist roads and away from monasteries, small, concrete bungalows have emerged or are under construction in the TAR (Observations #15; USDOS 30 March 2021). The ones that I spotted were all rigidly laid out in rows, facing the road. Some were painted, while others were not (or not yet). Chinese flags flew over most of them. The settlements' cold aesthetic gave me the impression of standing in front of lifeless and spiritless model villages (Observations #15). The guides are happy to explain that these new buildings are for nomads, who are offered the choice of settling down in "comfortable villages with modern facilities" or of remaining nomads (Observations #15). However, this account does not correspond with the testimony of nomads collected in Switzerland, who stated that they had no choice (USDOS 30 March 2021). The free, prior and informed consent that the Chinese authorities claim to have received from the nomads was, in fact, based on misinformation provided by government officials. Furthermore, two witnesses said that, even though they feel disheartened about having their traditional way of life taken away, the nomads are told to pretend to be happy when Chinese officials come to visit their new village. Some may receive money if they tell passing tourists that they are free and happy (Interviews #2, #21). The Chinese government seems to have little concern for nomads' long-term well-being and opportunities. Once they are settled, minimal assistance may be provided to nomads in certain areas, such as language teaching and cultivation training (SODNAMKYID/SULEK 2017:144–145), but such efforts must be sustained to be effective. During our study, none of our nomad interviewees mentioned such initiatives. The drastic change in lifestyle was traumatic, and with meagre financial resources and little to no life experience in cities, their prospects were bleak. Overall, the interviewees did not consider themselves as having received a better education after renouncing nomadism (for themselves or their children), but they did agree that healthcare was more accessible. Nonetheless, they do not think that their overall living standards have improved.

As regards the CCP's second justification, Tibetan interviewees are doubtful about the relevance of the settlement of nomads for the preservation of Tibet's natural environment. As Cencetti explains, the PRC wants to clear grassland from human activities to revitalise the soil, but, at the same time, settlement villages exacerbate the damage done by fencing and the division of land. Moreover, nomads, with their ancestral knowledge and experience, reckon that settlements should be avoided and that pre-1950 husbandry practices should be privileged (CENCETTI 2011:45). Xiangmei and Ahamed remark that nomads also had to cope with the dissolution of their communities (XIANGMEI/AHAMED 2018). The authors explain that under the propaganda and policy campaign *Comfortable Housing, Build a New Socialist Countryside,* "more than 2.6 million people – three-fourths of the entire population of the TAR were or will be moved into new houses" (XIANGMEI/AHAMED 2018; HRW 2013). The remaining explanation for this policy is the one proposed by Tibetans: most settlements of nomads are enforced (Interviews #2, #8, #11, #12, #13, #19; CENCETTI 2011:45; SODNAMKY-ID/SULEK 2017:139; USDOS 30 March 2021), probably as a means of monitoring them and planning their patriotic re-education. The nomads regret that the CCP does not demonstrate genuine interest in improving their living conditions, and, as a consequence, they believe it is only an excuse to reduce, or eradicate, nomadism. One former nomad lived on a grassland that initially housed 1,000 nomadic families. Now, he says, there are only 200 left (Interview #6). The problematic situation nomads face shows the CCP's failure, or unwillingness, to develop an economy that could support the growing urban population, while, at the same time, sustaining farmers in rural settlements and nomads on their grass-lands. The PRC does not value nomads' skills and overlooks their knowledge in preserving their ecological environment. Cencetti explains that, since the nomads have insufficient command of Chinese and Eng-lish, and therefore little to no access to academic scientific discourse, their knowledge is seen as unscientific and, thus, is ignored (CENCETTI 2011:47). Moreover, with the decline of the Tibetan language, nomads' skills are further endangered. As Nic Craith explains: "When languages die, traditional knowledge concerning the local environment and its species is also lost." (NIC CRAITH 2010:54). This is a concern for Tibet's natural environment, as well as a violation of nomads' rights and freedom.

> *We [nomads] are told by the Chinese to pretend to be happy in our new houses when tourists or officials arrive. But in our hearts, we are miserable. We lost our animals and our freedom. The propaganda pretends that we nomads are lucky to have pretty houses, but we are sad in our heart. It's like a prison. This is not a nomadic life.* (Interview #2)

> *What is currently dramatic is the situation of the nomads. The Chinese government wants them to settle down. They created reserves for nomads, or rather ghettos. I heard in 2018, that about 15% of nomads were relocated in these villages. For nomads, it's no longer a life.* (Interview # 6)

I was a pure nomad. I had no field and didn't work with farmers. We had sheep, yaks, dris, goats and dzo. We sold summer grass [caterpillar fungus], which grows abundantly in Tibet. But we had to pay heavy taxes for the cheese and butter we produced. During a conference [patriotic re-education], the Chinese ate one of our yaks but did not pay for it. They just left the skin and organs. (Interview #11)

We had 80 yaks. We also sold "Yartsa gunbu" [caterpillar fungus]. It is a very important source of income for nomads. It's a medicinal grass, very expensive, we sell it mainly to the Chinese. (Interview #19)

The Tibetans interviewed are concerned with the deterioration of Tibet's ecological environment. Buddhists have great respect for all living and non-living beings. Polluting the environment demonstrates a lack of respect and consideration for "the holiness of nature" (Interview #3). Tibetans need to keep Tibet's sacred lakes and mountains, the homes of Buddhist deities, unsullied. Lakes may have a divinatory purpose in the appointment of lamas. One of the tests that led to the Dalai Lama's nomination was indeed a vision in a lake (DALAI LAMA 2016:26). One witness says that disputes frequently occur when Tibetans see Chinese migrants or tourists fishing recreationally, an activity they view as disrespectful towards their faith and values (Interview #16). "As Buddhists", adds another interviewee, "Tibetans don't kill animals for pleasure. If we eat meat, it cannot be small animals. One yak is enough for a while." (Interview #3). The exploitation of Tibet's natural environment is a source of conflict. In remote areas across the TAR, countless trees, mostly pines, can be spotted planted in rows. During my trip, I asked my guides what they were used for, and I was told they were part of the PRC's "one million trees project", a program that is above all ecological (Observations #15). However, the explanations given by the interviewees were not quite the same. According to them, the purpose of planting those "one million trees" across Tibet in mostly deserted areas is instead to protect the PRC against flooding. They explained that, over the years, to meet the PRC's demand for wood and precious metals, Tibetan forests were overexploited and cut down to make way for the extraction of Tibet's natural resources and, notably, the construction of major road infrastructure projects. Chinese interventions have disrupted the environment's equilibrium, and with the ice melting from the Himalaya glaciers and increasingly heavy rains, floods have become a recurrent problem. Some witnesses add that if the PRC wants to plant its one million trees, it is not in order to sustain Tibetan forestry for the sake of Tibetans, but to fulfil the economic necessities of the PRC (Interviews #3, #4, #11, #13). One witness states that, in a place called Dege, in around 1995–1996, forests were excessively exploited by Chinese contractors. For three years, trees were cut down, "even big millennium trees" (Interview #13), and thrown into the Yellow River, or *Machu*, which was at that time used as a means of transportation to the PRC. Tibetans, who also needed wood, "were not allowed to take any, or they were shot." (Interview #13). Thus, the "one million trees project" has a less savoury backstory, when seen from the Tibetan side. One witness deplores the considerable deterioration of nature: "for 30 years, China exploited and destroyed the mountains and our landscapes. Nature can't survive if we take everything, it's a natural disaster", citing a place called Dzongsa as an example, where the extensive extraction of gold, copper and silver, along with other metals, significantly changed the landscape (Interview #13). Tibet is fortunate to have an abundance of natural resources, but the main beneficiaries of their exploitation are in the PRC. This is compounded by the militarisation of large areas of territories (Observations #15) whose activities further damage Tibet's natural environment, showing contempt for Tibetans' spiritual affiliation with their lands.

China says the development in Tibet is for our benefit. This is propaganda. In reality, 70% of economic benefits are for China. The remaining 30% may stay in Tibet, but it doesn't mean it is for Tibetans. (Interview #13)

The Chinese were taking the gold and destroying the landscapes, Tibetans were excluded. In 2014, Tibetans tried to protest. Clashes started with the Chinese police and some Tibetans were killed. (Interview #20)

We are all equals in terms of suffering. We are all looking for happiness. This is why we must do our utmost not to harm anyone. This is a common value between human rights and Buddhism. For Buddhists though, it extends to all beings, not only humans. Hence, our concern for the protection of the environment. (Interview #22)

For the Chinese authorities, any disagreement from the Tibetans is considered as political and attributed to foreign forces, even pleading for the preservation of our environment. (Interview #23)

Tibet's environment is deteriorating. The artist explains:

"There are no more trees, the snow is melting and the ground is drying up and becoming hostile to human and animal life. Chinese clouds are very present, but cannot hide the ongoing ecological disaster from the international community."

Anonymous Tibetan artist, Switzerland, 2020.

Conclusion

A cultural practice deserves protection when it is experienced as an expression of individuals and communities (MEYER-BISCH/BIDAULT 2010:67). Basic needs are the same for everyone; it is the means of satisfying them that differ according to our cultural background. For Tibetans, Buddhism holds a central place in their lives, and the freedom to express their faith and identity is inseparable from their well-being. Tibet is culturally Buddhist, and Tibetans, whether devoted believers or not, were raised in an environment imbued with Buddhist peace-oriented values. This is what the CCP is trying to disrupt. The forced assimilation being imposed on Tibet is not about isolated acts of violence. It is widespread and systemic violence committed over the long term. Since Buddhism plays a central role in Tibetans' lives, it is no accident that the CCP spends a lot of energy meddling in Buddhist affairs. By usurping spiritual leadership and by making it difficult for Tibetans to fulfil spiritual requirements, the Party seeks to turn them away from Buddhism and to weaken their resistance in order to advance its interests (LEMKIN 1944:85, 89–90). Tibetans' life choices, cultural expressions and educational opportunities are restricted. The CCP is notably eager to enrol children in Chinese schools, to transfer teachers and to settle nomads in order to extend its influence and authority (LEMKIN 1944:84, 89, 90). The CCP also undermines national feelings, by restricting the use of the Tibetan language and by controlling cultural activities. It deprives Tibetans of the right of free access to sources of knowledge, as well as of the right to enjoy and protect their cultural heritage without interference from the authorities (LEMKIN 1944:84). Finally, Tibetans' spiritual ties to their environment are disregarded, and nomads in particular have little say regarding their ancestral territories and resources. As reported by the USDOS, in 2020, "[f]orced assimilation was pursued by promoting the influx of non-Tibetans to traditionally Tibetan areas, expanding the domestic tourism industry, forcibly resettling and urbanizing nomads and farmers, weakening Tibetan language education in public schools, and weakening monasteries' role in Tibetan society, especially with respect to religious education." (USDOS May 2021). Ecocide should also be mentioned, given the damage or destruction of Tibet's environment, which particularly impacts nomads' livelihoods – and thus their way of life and survival (SHORT 2016:38). Cultural diversity may be blamed for social instability, but, in reality, the problem lies with intolerance and the belief in a superior identity that one tries to enforce. It is harmful to believe that a unique identity can, and should, be obtained (SEN 2006:xv–xvi). By controlling all means of cultural expressions and violating cultural rights, the CCP seeks to undermine Tibetan identity claims that it associates with nationalism and separatism, as well as to disrupt national unity amongst Tibetans in order to enforce its own national sensibilities (LEMKIN 1944:83–84). Tibetans are also required to cooperate with the CCP in the hope of being awarded privileges, such as educational and employment opportunities (LEMKIN 1944:82–83, 86). For the others, their participation in economic and cultural life is made difficult, if not dangerous, by exposing them to discrimination, marginalisation and persecution.

4

THE RIGHT TO KNOW
AND THE MONOPOLY OF TRUTH

Introduction

The testimonies underline the importance Tibetans attach to their history, both for the preservation of their collective memory and as a central element of their identity. Yet, memory and history, while intertwined, ought to be distinguished. As Schnapper writes, memory "can be fashioned independently of the diversity or opposition of national histories" (SCHNAPPER 2008:71). History, however, cannot be fashioned after models of historical propaganda, which put the state, and not the people, at the centre of its narrative. The CCP presents itself as the sole arbiter of truth, seeking to impose its own version of Tibet's history. The right to know the past, one of the four interconnected key pillars of Dealing with the Past (DwP), along with the right to reparation, the right to justice and the guarantee of non-recurrence, is of central importance in the fight against the forced amnesia of past atrocities and impunity. These four pillars give priority to victims and survivors (Swisspeace 2016:6). History can play an essential role in promoting peace by preventing misinformation and prejudice. However, silencing or manipulating it makes the past a powerful weapon of oppression and prevents accountability mechanisms that victims, survivors of abuse and their families deserve and are entitled to. This chapter will focus on the

CCP's attempts to silence any reminders of the past that do not serve its political interests, while consolidating and materialising its version of Tibet's history through tourism, monuments and commemorations. It will also explain how, and why, the Party seeks to undermine and ultimately replace the Dalai Lama's spiritual leadership.

[Annapurna]. *The 4 Way Test of things we think, say and do:*

1. Is it the TRUTH? 2. Is it FAIR to all concerned? 3. Will it build GOODWILL and BETTER FRENDSHIP? 4. Will it be BENEFICIAL to all concerned?

Inspiring message from Nepal. *Morel, Nepal, 2015.*

4.1 Distorting History

2007 Declaration on the Rights of Indigenous Peoples. Article 8, Article 13(1), Article 15, Article 16.

If people [in Switzerland] find out that the history of Tibet is controversial, it's already a victory for Tibetans. China has failed to assert its version as the absolute truth. If people forget there's a conflict, two versions of Tibet's history, our cause will be lost. (Interview #5)

China wants Tibetans to work for them and not to think about anything else. If you start thinking, it's very difficult, and that's when the trouble starts. (Interview #9)

In Tibet, we can't see the world and think for ourselves. Everything is censored: Google, WhatsApp, YouTube, Facebook. (Interview #18)

It is the responsibility of every Tibetan to transmit the history of what happened, whether the situation deteriorates or improves. (Interview #24)

Tibetans have little freedom regarding their life paths, and their very own histories are under scrutiny. The CCP has placed the narration of Tibetans' history under the strict and exclusive monopoly of official Communist historiographers (BONNIN/HALL 2007:52–53). Historical accuracy and fairness are secondary. What matters is whether the interpretation given satisfies the CCP's ideology (CHANGCHING 2015:25). In order to serve its political interests and justify the occupation, the Party uses its own narratives to maintain the fear of "social instability" and to justify the use of force, while denying responsibility for, or even the existence of, violence. It propagates stereotypes and misconceptions about Tibetans and Tibet, with widespread disinformation campaigns. It has made history a privileged tool in its long-lasting assimilation project and ground its arguments in the assumption that Tibet had long been Chinese, a narrative that cannot be challenged. Their political, rather than historical, analysis of the past is required to glorify the PRC and legitimise the Party's authority over Tibet, while repressive measures, failures and violence are carefully concealed. In this regard, the works of Epstein (1915–2005), a Polish-born naturalised Chinese writer, and of Strong (1885–1970), an American journalist and advocate of Communism, are interesting, since they are two early, well-known Western-born sympathisers and promoters of the CCP's narrative about Tibet. However, the focus here will be on another book bought in Lhasa, *L'histoire du Tibet,* written by Qingying (2004). It recounts the CCP's version of Tibet's history and demonstrates the oblivion into which past violent events have fallen. The Party, and thus Qingying, focuses on events before 1959, with a particular emphasis on Tibet as de facto belonging to the PRC. It describes Tibet's allegedly backward society and the CCP's unequivocally "peaceful" achievements. Moreover, as explained below, the Party realigns and readjusts its speech – and history – whenever necessary to justify the "liberation" of Tibetans. The status of Tibet is the subject of heated debate. Following the fall of the Qing dynasty in 1911–1912, the International Commission of Jurists recognised that Tibet was not under the PRC's sovereignty (ICJ 1959:98). Correspondingly, Tibet's independence was proclaimed in 1913 by the 13th Dalai Lama (1876–1933). The Tibetan testimonies highlighted the view that the evidence of their independence depends as much on Tibet's history and territory, as on its unique cultural identity, in the form of its language, traditions and moral values (Interviews #1, #7, #12, #13, #18, #22, #23). They explain that Tibetans culturally distinguish themselves from Han Chinese, but more importantly, they feel that, morally speak, they stand in stark contrast with the Party's ideology and actions. The predominance of the cultural element in Tibetans' conception of independence is, undoubtedly, the reason why the CCP sees the Tibetans' identity claims and their calls for the preservation of Tibet's cultural heritage as representing political threats. The Party thus seeks to undermine their identity, in order to break their sense of unity.

In the PRC, an era "is defined by the term that each imperial house remained in power." (CHANGCHING/SEYMOUR 2015:vii). Consequently, at best, the CCP claims that Tibet has been part of the PRC since the Yuan dynasty (13th century). More often, though, the Party settles on the notion that it has been so "since ancient times" (Interview

#16; Sperling 2009:33; Observations #15), even if its arguments remain unclear and unconvincing (CHAYET 2008:37–38). Despite the proclaimed reunification and liberation, the military takeover of Tibet was motivated by the natural resources with which this vast territory is endowed. Its exploitation could generate substantial revenues for the PRC. Furthermore, the occupation addressed the CCP's security concerns with regard to the Western territories. In the early years of the occupation, the rhetoric of the CCP focused on the liberation of Tibetans from imperialists, i.e. from the Americans and the British. In other words, Tibet was allegedly under foreign occupation and had to be "freed", or rather occupied, by the PRC instead. Hence, the CCP declared Tibet to be part of the PRC, in order to resolve this contradiction. It underlined how peacefully the PLA liberated Tibetans. By denying that it resorted to military violence, the CCP seeks to establish Tibetans' consent to the Chinese occupation and to membership of the PRC. The Party also stressed the necessity of the PLA's intervention in order to save Tibetans from their backward society plagued by serfdom. The CCP still propagates a very bleak picture of Tibet before 1949, referring to the majority of Tibetans as impoverished, mistreated and tortured serfs. In an exchange of correspondence between the Swiss former Federal Councillor Willy Spühler and Chang Wen-Chin, Minister's Assistant of Foreign Affairs in 1973, the CCP reaffirmed its rightful ownership over Tibet and stated that the latter was granted great autonomy. In the diplomatic document, the Chinese representative portrayed Tibetan society before the occupation in gruesome terms. According to him, Tibet had lived under brutal serfdom and was a territory where "We killed people for our own pleasure." (SFA dodis.ch/37714 1973:6). In Qingying's book, we find several photographs of alleged Tibetan serfs suffering from torture, famine, poverty and forced labour, without any metadata (such as photographer, date, location, context) being provided to legitimate them. The captions under the pictures give a simplistic interpretation that aligns with the

CCP's indisputable assertion that Tibetans lived under extreme distress before the occupation. Photographs are presented as unquestionable evidence that mirror the truth (QINGYING 2004:139–143). Although Tibetan serfdom is a widely accepted fact amongst sympathisers of the CCP, on the international level, scholars disagree about the very existence of serfdom and feudalism in Tibet (BARNETT 2008:82). If Tibetans experienced inequality and exploitation before the Chinese occupation, they remained united in their Buddhist faith and supported their religious institutions (SHAKYA 1999:143). Yet, the PLA presented themselves as the saviours of all Tibetans. Its takeover enabled the CCP to undertake its colonisation or "civilising mission" in Tibet. More recently, the CCP has adjusted its discourse to underline its essential role in Tibet, especially the TAR, notably with respect to the region's economic development and the preservation of its natural environment.

In its narrative of Tibet's history, the CCP shows no interest in the victims' fate and the trauma they endured. The violence of major historical events is cast into oblivion with disconcerting impunity. Qingying writes that Tibetans from Eastern Tibet were "full of joy and felt encouraged" at the announcement of the foundation of the PRC, in 1949 (QINGYING 2004:112). The author refers to the battle of Chamdo in 1950 as a peaceful liberation and explains that when the PLA entered the city, the army was welcomed by monks and inhabitants (QINGYING 2004:121). According to Qingying, the Dalai Lama addressed a telegram to Mao on 24 October 1951, in which he expressed the unanimous support of the Tibetan government and its people regarding the 17-Point Agreement. Furthermore, the Dalai Lama allegedly stated that the Tibetan people would help the PLA to "consolidate national defence, drive imperialist forces out of Tibet, and safeguard the territorial integrity and sovereignty of the homeland." (QINGYING 2004:134). It is not possible to verify the validity of the statement, as no reference is given. One of the most striking examples of the distortion of history concerns the 1959 uprising that resulted in a mass atrocity. Qingying refers it as an incident launched by reactionaries, who wanted the Dalai Lama to leave Tibet (QINGYING 2004:147–148). In the correspondence addressed to Willy Spühler, Chang Wen-Chin states that India had "used lamas and large landowners to trigger a rebellion in 1959" (SFA dodis.ch/37704 1973:6), which is reported to have failed very quickly following the lack of support from the Tibetan population (SFA dodis.ch/37714 1973:6). The uprising had reportedly caused the deaths of 545 people amongst the Tibetan "rebel armed force" (QINGYING 2004:151). According to Qingying, the Dalai Lama had written in a letter to General Tan Guanshan, from the Tibet Work Committee, stating that the reactionaries, while pretending to protect him, were engaged in activities that threatened his safety, and thus, "sought to get rid of them." (QINGYING 2004:149–150). Regarding the Dalai Lama's exile, he asserts that the PLA had no intention of hindering his escape (QINGYING 2004:150).

> *I had known the Chinese occupation since childhood. Life was very hard. We did not have enough to eat, our clothes were not suitable for the seasons or for our work, Chinese law was arbitrary. My parents were often absent because of work. I was educated by my paternal grandparents. My whole family suffered greatly under the occupation. After work, in the evening, my father had to go to political sessions, the thamzing. These sessions were greatly feared by Tibetans. My father was beaten up because the Chinese thought he was a resistance fighter. He was also sent to prison, as were my great uncle and paternal grandfather, who both died in prison. The abusive treatment of the Chinese towards Tibetans became normal, we were used to it.* (Interview #24)

This testimony gives an example of a *thamzing*, which was meant to force Tibetans to denounce the so-called three evils of the old society, namely the Tibetan government, aristocratic estate holders and monasteries (Shakya 1999:248–249). The Party protects its monopoly over history with sanctions and measures aiming to suppress any information that might challenge the CCP's historical discourse. In February 1984, for instance, the monk Geshe Lobsang Wangchuk was condemned to 18 years in prison for having written leaflets on Tibetan history and its independence (AI 1987:169). In January 2015, the Internet became the prime target in the CCP's censorship campaign. The Party notably shut down 133 WeChat accounts it considered vectors of information "distorting the history of the Communist Party and national history". The repression also greatly affected education. The same year, foreign textbooks were banned, and warnings were issued against the infiltration of "hostile forces" in universities (AI 2015/2016). The Party pushes the development of mass tourism, particularly in the TAR, as a financially lucrative propaganda method.

4.2 Heritage Interpretations

> 2007 Declaration on the Rights of Indigenous Peoples. Article 8, Article 11, Article 12(1), Article 31.

States have the responsibility to protect cultural heritage and ensure that monuments and commemorations are peace-oriented, aim to help the healing process of survivors of atrocities and promote tolerance between peoples, so as to prevent further violence by combatting impunity through collective amnesia. Cultural heritage connects past and future generations. The destruction or alteration of historic and religious sites, the imposed amnesia in relation to atrocities and any onslaught against "the memories of the witnesses of freedoms" are violations of cultural rights (MEYER-BISCH/BIDAULT 2010:47). They are a humiliating and painful reminder of the disdain the CCP has for Tibetan victims, survivors and their descendants. As stated in Chapter 1, the CCP dissolved Tibet and created the TAR, marking the incorporation of the occupied territory into the PRC (LEMKIN 1944:82). Regarding the cultural heritage in Tibet, interviewees state that although the Party preserves selected historical buildings and promotes some local traditions, it is only for the purposes of mass tourism and propaganda, which the interviewees feel contributes to the denigration of their cultural heritage and beliefs. Witnesses explain that the CCP builds new monuments, adapts Tibetan architecture to suit Chinese taste and tends to destroy historical buildings rather than renovating them according to local customs and specificities. Aesthetics and entertainment are prioritised for touristic consumption, to the detriment of Tibetan Buddhist traditions and values (Interviews #8, #9, #17, #21). Therefore, some feel that the CCP has locked Tibet, and its cultural heritage, behind bars (Interviews #8, #9, #21) that it "tries to hide with golden paint" (Interviews #8). They also underline the misbehaviour and misinformation observed in some tourists. In more prominent monasteries, such as Ganzi Sertar Larung Gar Buddhist Institute and Taktsang Lhamo Kirti Monastery, sky burials "are like shows for Chinese tourists who invade holy sites to take pictures of the so-called barbaric Tibetan customs" (Interview #17).

> *They [Han Chinese] don't respect our holy sites. They walk on prayer flags or wear them to laugh. They also steal holy stones with ancient Tibetan mantras. They play with our culture.* (Interview #13)

> *Our body is a waste when we die. Sky burial is a blessing, a generous act to offer it to animals. I don't understand why Chinese come just to watch it, Tibetans don't.* (Interview #21)

The CCP retains a firm grip on the Tibetan cultural heritage, in order to avoid losing control over an evolving culture and traditional life. Consequently, the CCP is likely to freeze Tibetan cultural heritage in time. Rare are Tibetan historical monuments like the Potala Palace (UNESCO World Heritage List since 1994) that have not been destroyed or excessively altered (Observations #15). One interviewee considers that the significant and rapid changes in Tibet's cultural environment by the Chinese authorities are difficult to accept and makes "cities and especially Lhasa look Chinese" (Interview #9). This witness explains they do not need all that "decoration". The use of natural products, which are traditional in Tibet, should be privileged, which is not the case (Interview #9). A former monk also expresses his dismay, as for him, before the Chinese occupation, "Potala Palace was like a paradise, only exceptional people could access it. Now there is no peace of mind, and what the Chinese do with our heritage is all about decoration" (Interview #14).

> *All that decoration. It upsets us. Tourists need to know our reality that is hidden behind the pretty walls.* (Interview #8)

> *This monument [the Peaceful Liberation of Tibet monument], I think it's sad. It's a holy site but now looks Chinese and we can't say anything. Before, the site looked very Tibetan. It was covered with flowers.* (Interview #9)

> *We don't need all these Chinese products; we don't like materialism.* (Interview #21)

Lhasa. The Peaceful Liberation of Tibet monument (2002) at Potala Square, was not designed to commemorate past atrocities. Rather, it celebrates the PLA's takeover, which was supposedly welcomed by Tibetans.

Morel, Lhasa, TAR, 2019.

4.3 The Dalai Lama, His Succession and the CCP

2007 Declaration on the Rights of Indigenous Peoples. Article 13, Article 15, Article 18, Article 31, Article 33(1), Article 36(1),

The CCP aims to enforce collective amnesia, not only of past events but also of Tibetans perceived as a threat to its interests. Along with the physical absence of Tibetans, due to enforced disappearances or exile, the CCP may also have recourse to measures to erase their memory, or *damnatio memoriae,* i.e. condemnation of memory. Taken in a broad and more contemporary sense, this implies a strategy seeking to remove any traces, in history and people's mind, of the existence of someone. Tibetan interviewees consider the Dalai Lama as their spiritual leader and as the rightful "King of Tibet, the head and the heart of Tibetans." (Interviews #1, #16). They pray for his return to Tibet and believe it would bring peace and freedom for Tibetans. One foreign witness confirms that Tibetans' faith in the Dalai Lama remains intact in Tibet: "when the situation gets worse, I feel they support him with an ever-increasing fervour." (Interview #6). A large number of Tibetans are still profoundly affected by his exile in 1959 and remain devoted to him. The CCP responds to the Tibetans' loyalty to the Dalai Lama by launching defamation campaigns, aimed at discrediting him as a leader and as a spiritual role model, while also labelling his followers as threats to the nation. The Party denigrates his rank by referring to him as the "Dalai" and "his clique" (i.e. the CTA) and poses him as a "splittist", a traitor, the enemy of the PRC, and thus, of all Tibetans. As Barnett explains, "the constant press attacks on him were a sign that he was now to be regarded as a religious fraud as well as a political outcast" (BARNETT 1999:188). The CCP wants Tibetans to believe, or at least forcibly adhere to, its own version of absolute truth regarding the Dalai Lama, which causes great suffering, especially among nuns and monks (Chapter 3). The Party wants the Dalai Lama to slowly fade away from

Tibetans' collective memory. It was explained, notably in Chapter 3, how the Chinese educational curriculum excluded any mention of sensitive topics, such as the Dalai Lama, and sought to replace him by party leaders through patriotic re-education (Interviews #2, #13, #19). Consequently, young people who do not benefit from intergenerational transmission of knowledge have little chance to hear about him (Interviews #9, #10), apart from through the CCP's relentless propaganda. The CCP tightened its policies regarding the iconography of the Dalai Lama in Tibet. Starting from April 1996, photographs of him were prohibited from being displayed in public areas. The ban was then extended to households. According to the interviewees, even though pictures, videos and books of the Dalai Lama were officially banned in 1996, punishments were imposed for possessing such objects even before the mid-1990s (Interviews #6, #14, #17, #23). Furthermore, the CCP seeks to isolate the Dalai Lama at the international level and to end his influence not only in Tibet, but abroad as well (CECC 2010:214).

> *When I was little, I didn't know the Dalai Lama; I didn't understand who he was. I thought he might be some kind of a big statue. I discovered the truth as I grew older.* (Interview #9)

> *Older people told me about the 14ᵗʰ Dalai Lama, and I realised that China wasn't that good for us. My Dad explained me everything about the Dalai Lama and Tibet. We had a hidden picture of the Dalai Lama in our family. I was in shock; I had to believe the truth, but it was difficult. At first, I was a bit angry, but then I was happy to know we had a great leader and a government.* (Interview #10)

> *A Tibetan sat next to me and, in a low voice, asked me if I had recent photos of the Dalai Lama. He then told me he only saw old pictures of him and, to his regret, didn't know what he looked like today. He said that he missed his voice, although he confessed to not being sure of really remembering it. After a while, I started searching for photos of the Dalai Lama on my phone, using my VPN, and handed it to him. He was close to tears, but his face lit up. He stood up, his hands pressed togeth-*

er, and started praying. It didn't last very long but this anec-
dote will stay with me for good. (Interview #16)

A friend's cousin was a monk. He had a large photo of the Da-
lai Lama in his room. Usually, monks don't let strangers in;
they are afraid of spies. As I had visited him a few times with
his cousin, he trusted me. He died just over a year later. He
threw himself into the freezing Kyichu river for fear of repris-
als, because someone saw the photograph and denounced him
to the authorities. (Interview #17)

The physical absence of the Dalai Lama from Tibet, the CCP's attacks against his reputation and dignity, and its efforts to keep his activities hidden, especially from young people, are all meant to bring about
his enforced disappearance from Tibetans' lives. Furthermore, in an
attempt to undermine his leadership within Tibetan Buddhism, the CCP
is increasingly interfering in religious affairs. On 14 May 1995, Gedhun
Choekyi Nyima, aged 6, was recognised by the Dalai Lama as the reincarnation of the 10th Panchen Lama. The enforced disappearance of the
child three days after his nomination represented a political low for the
CCP, aggravated by its explicit refusal to provide information on his
whereabouts to the international community (OHCHR 2012:41). The
Party appointed its own 11th Panchen Lama instead, Gyancain Norbu,
and has subsequently forced Tibetans to recognise him, notably during
patriotic re-education in monasteries (Chapter 3). Primarily directed
against the Dalai Lama's spiritual leadership, the enforced disappearance[5] of Gedhun Choekyi Nyima had a lengthy, far-reaching and painful

---

[5] In Article 2 of the International Convention for the Protection of All Persons
from Enforced Disappearance (ICPPED), adopted in 2006, enforced disappearance implies "[a]rrest, detention, abduction or any other form of deprivation of
liberty by agents   of the State or by persons or groups of persons acting with
the authorization, support or acquiescence of the State, followed   by a refusal
to acknowledge the deprivation of liberty or by concealment of the fate or
whereabouts of the disappeared person,   which place such a person outside

impact on Tibetans in Tibet, as well as the Tibetan diaspora and sympathisers worldwide. To this day, the PRC still refuses to provide information on his whereabouts. The CCP seeks to replace Tibetan religious leaders by its own figureheads, as it did in the case of the Panchen Lama, going so far as to demand that Tibetans "worship the five Chinese leaders" (Interview #19). In 2007, the PRC's State Administration of Religious Affairs No 5, or *Measures on the Management of the Reincarnation of Living Buddhas in Tibetan Buddhism*, further denigrates spirituality and people's beliefs. The order aims to regulate the management of reincarnations and to define the procedures for identifying living Buddhas. Article 2, in particular, reveals the political objectives of the order. It stipulates that, in order to be authorised, a reincarnation must serve Chinese national unity. No foreign interference by an individual or organisation is tolerated, implying that the 14th Dalai Lama has no say over his own reincarnation. The 15th Dalai Lama will have to reincarnate in the PRC and respect Chinese rules and laws. On 30 January 2020, the Senate and House of Representatives of the United States of America approved the modification and reauthorisation of the Tibetan Policy Act of 2002. The document notably underlines that reincarnations of Buddhist leaders must remain "solely within the Tibetan Buddhist faith community, in accordance with the inalienable right to religious freedom" (TPSA H.R.4331 2020:8). In response to statements by the Dalai Lama and the US government, the CCP, through its state-run newspaper *Global Times*, has expressed outrage at what the Party sees as "gross interference in China's internal affairs" (Global Times 2020). In stating that the Tibetan spiritual leader's reincarnation is an internal Chinese matter, the CCP once again chooses to ignore the fact that the

---

the protection of the law." Committee on Enforced Disappearances, *International Convention for the Protection of All Persons from Enforced Disappearance*, www.ohchr.org/en/hrbodies/ced/pages/conventionced.aspx [25.06.2021].

Dalai Lama is an eminent spiritual figure, who is recognised internationally and who inspires people across the globe, well beyond the confines of Tibet and the Tibetan diaspora. His succession is a matter of central importance for Tibetan Buddhism, which is practised in many countries. Consequently, the Chinese cannot retain an exclusive say over the reincarnation of the 15th Dalai Lama and the management of affairs related to Tibetan Buddhism. If the CCP goes ahead and imposes a 15th Dalai Lama on Tibetans on the basis of its own laws, rules and interests, this will merely exacerbate the conflict in Tibet and further place Tibetans in jeopardy. They will be forced to comply with the CCP's dictates and endure deep moral pain, of the kind felt by nuns and monks forced to condemn the Dalai Lama, by recognising the CCP-appointed 11th Panchen Lama (Chapter 3.1), or risk persecution. The CCP also dedicates significant energy to censoring the Dalai Lama beyond its borders. The Party attempts to interfere in the Dalai Lama's activities and official visits. The success of its economic blackmail depends on the docility, and economic interests, of foreign states. Yet, the Dalai Lama and the Tibetan diaspora play a crucial role in voicing their experiences as a challenge to that the absolute truth the CCP is attempting to dictate and impose on the world.

> *We only hope for the return of the Dalai Lama, because it would mean freedom for Tibetans.* (Interview #7)

> *The return of the Dalai Lama to Tibet is a deep wish for Tibetans. In my opinion, it is not only about his physical return. It is a call for a resolution of the conflict between Tibet and China.* (Interview #22)

Beijing Road before the transformation of Lhasa. *Anonymous photographer, Lhasa, TAR, between 2007 and 2009.*

Intensive construction of concrete residential buildings, disfiguring the urban and natural landscape of Lhasa and its surroundings. *Morel, Lhasa, TAR, 2019.*

Conclusion

With its monopoly of truth, the CCP pretends to foster shared values and ideology, but in reality denies Tibetans' freedom of thought, conscience and religion. The national memory the CCP is trying to create and to impose by force glorifies the state, enforces collective amnesia about past abuses and heightens impunity. Investigating the past and the willingness to address grievances are essential for a peaceful future. As Schnapper puts it, "[t]he past is not to be negated or blotted out. Answering for and transcending the past is the key to being present in the present and to envisaging the future." (SCHNAPPER 2008:71). Tibetans and Han Chinese have the right to access knowledge, as well as to pluralistic, critical and objective interpretations of their history. The Party's interference in the collective memory of both Tibetans and Han Chinese is a direct violation of their cultural rights, given that "the right to memory is constitutive of the right to heritage." (MEYER-BISCH/BIDAULT 2010:47). Under the CCP, history is no longer the reminder of past atrocities that should be fought against, but a propaganda tool to serve political ambitions. To further undermine Tibetan unity, historic buildings, as symbols of Tibet's past and Tibetan former society, were destroyed, damaged or altered to suit Chinese tastes (LEMKIN 1944:84). Furthermore, new monuments and commemorations were introduced to materialise the CCP's version of truth. The Party's attempts to silence the Dalai Lama by discrediting him and interfering in Tibetan Buddhist affairs, in order to disrupt his religious influence on Tibetans (LEMKIN 1944:89). Although already mentioned in Chapter 3, the willingness of the CCP to usurp religious leadership positions, including that of the Dalai Lama, aims to "weaken the spiritual resistance" of Tibetans and lead them to devote themselves solely to the CCP (LEMKIN 1944:89–90).

> *Truth is powerful. We have the truth; you can't hide or eliminate it. I hope Swiss people will support it.* (Interview #4)

5

DEALING WITH TRAUMAS
AND THE PAIN OF UNCERTAINTY

Introduction

As O'Keefe states, some cultural groups, such as the Tibetans, have "lost much of their history to conquest, colonialism and the destruction of their societies. They now need to relearn who they are and where they come from." (O'KEEFE 1997:7). Tibetans must regain possession of their past to heal and help them embrace their future – and Tibet's future – on solid ground. The interviewees showed remarkable resilience and a capacity to stand back from Tibet's situation to inform, discern and explain their experiences. The spiritually rooted resilience of Tibetans entails tolerance towards suffering, the ability to limit its effects on one's life and, more importantly, the capacity to transform pain into compassion, and thus spiritual growth. Nevertheless, the situation remains unbearable, for some, who see in self-immolation the only way to express their despair and call for help. The testimonies collected also underline the necessity of encouraging the promotion of mutual understanding, tolerance and trust between Tibetans and Han Chinese. Based on Lederach's work on conflict transformation (LEDERACH 2003), opportunities will be suggested for encouraging authentic interactions between Tibetans and Han Chinese. The focus will be placed on potential opportunities to reduce discrimination and marginalisation in Tibet, as well as to prevent other forms of violence against Tibetans.

5.1 Self-immolations

It is psychologically damaging to prevent an entire population from expressing themselves and being who they are. Like other forms of protest described in this report, demonstrations respond to the emotional need of Tibetans to be recognised as free and unique human beings, and to express what is of value to them. As the testimonies show, a significant number of Tibetans must cope with the forced absences of relatives and friends. They also highlight the fact that devoted Tibetans are deeply affected by two ambiguous shared losses, that of the Dalai Lama and that of the 11th Panchen Lama. The leading expert on the concept of ambiguous loss, Dr Pauline Boss, describes it as an "unclear loss that defies closure" (BOSS 2006:xvii), characterised by the physical and, subsequently, gradual psychological disappearance of someone (BOSS 2006:1). It notably occurs when the circumstances of death remain unclear or when a person's fate following an enforced disappearance is unknown. In the absence of closure, the grieving process can remain closed off to those left behind, in which case the ambiguous loss becomes traumatic (BOSS 2006:xvii, xix, 1). Clinically, a trauma is an "overwhelming emotional experiences that cannot be coped with and integrated into the person's existing inner world." (MACEK 2014:4). Since they are not processed psychologically, traumatic events will be preserved in the same form as they were first experienced by the victim and be repeated if triggered by a stimulus (MACEK 2014:4). Macek further explains that family members of survivors of extreme violence can also experience "secondary experiences of violence." (MACEK 2014:6). Trauma can, therefore, be transmitted to the next generations who hear stories from their families or accounts from survivors and witnesses of abuses. The healing process of Tibetans is further impeded by the actions of the CCP, which continues to deny past and ongoing violence, and thus Tibetans' suffering. Tibetans are prevented from reuniting to commemorate painful events and from honouring the memory of victims. The difficulties in healing can make life unbearable for Tibetans. While the majority seek refuge in their faith and their power of resilience, some have recourse to extreme self-violence, in the hope of being heard and of relieving others, at one's own expense. The CTA has reported 157 self-immolations since 1998, of which the vast majority occurred in Tibet. As of the time of writing, the last self-immolation to have occurred was that of Yonton (24), a young former monk from Kirti Monastery, on 26 November 2019.

This drawing contains several messages, as the artist explains. There are references to the independence of Tibet proclaimed in 1913 by the 13th Dalai Lama and the rebellion of 1959. In the centre, the treasury, or *norbu*, represents the three provinces of Kham, Amdo and U-Tsang. The eyes are those of the Tibetans who mourn the loss of their lands and whose tears are accumulating in a pool. The name "Tibet" is written in Tibetan, in green letters to symbolise peace and the efforts of Tibetans to achieve it. Finally, the flames are a reminder of the self-immolations that have occurred since 2009. *Anonymous Tibetan artist, Switzerland, 2019.*

It's a sacrifice for others, they are so desperate to express themselves, they kill themselves even knowing life is beautiful and precious. They don't want to die. Often, they leave letters to explain why they did it. (Interview #21)

Self-immolations are an act of despair. A burn is a sharp pain that people can understand and may even have experienced to a lesser extent. It is thus a way of trying to make their pain understandable to the international community, but also to the Party. (Interview #23)

Self-immolations of Tibetans (ICT 2021)

1998–2019

- 157 self-immolations, including 129 men and 28 women:

- 125 of the 157 victims are known to have died following their protest

- 26 of the Tibetans who self-immolated were 18 or younger

- 25 were monks, or former monks, at Kirti Monastery in Ngaba

- 2 were nuns from Mame Dechen Chokorling Nunnery in Ngaba

- 10 occurred in India and Nepal, 7 of these died from their wounds

The first self-immolation occurred on 27 April 1998, in Delhi, India.

The interviewees explain that self-immolations are a desperate attempt to speak out and be heard. They believe that the protestors do not want to die, but see it as the last option available to them. In Chapter 3.1, it was explained that the distress of nuns and monks forced to criticise the Dalai Lama during patriotic re-education led some of them to contemplate suicide. A monk explains that such a situation must be distinguished from suicide by self-immolation. Tibetans who self-immolate are determined to die and plan their death. They may explicitly express their motivations, either in a letter or, more often, by crying them out during the immolation. In these cases, their recurring demands are the Dalai Lama's return in Tibet, religious freedom and the preservation of the Tibetan culture (Interview #22). However, for nuns and monks, the indoctrination and accusations they have been forced to endure have caused them deep moral conflict. If their pain has reached the limit of what they can endure, they refrain from suicide, strengthened by their faith and self-control (Interview #22). As Buddhists, Tibetans need to do whatever is necessary so as not to hurt anyone. Therefore, self-immolations are "a strong and symbolic act of protest, aiming to awaken public opinion without hurting others." (Interview #22). Golok Jigme considers that "we can only have compassion for the victims. Culpability is for the Party for not letting Tibetans express themselves." (Interview #23). According to one witness, the Chinese authorities' response is cold and severe. Treated as a terrorist act "an entire village can be punished after a self-immolation." (Interview #6; IRB 2020). The victims' relatives, including children, can be sentenced to imprisonment or patriotic re-education (HRW 2011). In 2016, Human Rights Watch reported the case of an 11-year-old boy who was jailed after the self-immolation of his father (HRW 2016). The CCP drafts and adopts new laws and instructions to criminalise self-immolations, as well as to prosecute victims and possibly even their relatives. If they die from their injuries, Tibetans are denied any traditional rituals. Prayers and homages for the victim are illegal, as are gestures of sympathy towards the family. The prohibition on commemorating the victims of self-immolations is another example of the violation of the right to memory. Sharing information on self-immolations with international partners, as well as mentioning them in Tibet, are also sanctioned.

> *The preoccupation of the CCP is its image, not the deaths of Tibetans. It is a terrorist regime that doesn't recognise that life is precious, and that all life must be protected. In 2012, a person I knew didn't want the authorities to take the body of a self-immolated Tibetan. So, he tried to take him away to offer him a ceremony. For this, he was sentenced to 10 years in jail.*
> (Interview #23)

5.2 Addressing Tibetans' Grievances: The Middle Way Approach

Until the early 1970s, Tibet's independence was a prime concern for the Dalai Lama and the CTA. However, in 1979, Deng Xiaoping expressed his willingness to engage in dialogue only if the CTA renounced any claims to independence (ROEMER 2010:83). What is known today as the Middle Way Approach (MWA), conceived by the Dalai Lama, is a policy "based on the principles of justice, compassion, non-violence, friendship and in the spirit of reconciliation" (DIIR 2016:1). This policy would maintain the "status quo in combination with an attempt to renew the dialogue with the PRC about Tibetan autonomy" (ROEMER 2010:85), and thus guarantee religious freedom. It seeks to address Tibetans' grievances and aims to promote and protect Tibetans' rights and freedoms. The efforts of the MWA aim to bring about peace-driven negotiations and to provide Tibetans with prompt relief. Specifically, this approach agrees to compromise and to renounce independence, in line with "Buddhist principles of avoiding extremes and instead, finding middle ground" for the benefit of both Tibetans and Han Chinese (DIIR 2018(1):225), while remaining within the scope of the Constitution of the PRC (DIIR 2016:20).

In his efforts to find a peaceful resolution for Tibet, the Dalai Lama presented his Five-Point Peace Plan in 1987 (Appendix E) at the United States Congregational Human Rights Caucus in Washington, on 21 September 1987. In his introduction, the Dalai Lama recalled that Tibet was an independent nation before the Chinese takeover. While stating that he had no intention of discussing Tibet's current status, the Dalai Lama emphasised "the obvious and undisputed fact that we Tibetans are a distinct people with our own culture, language, religion and history" (Appendix E). In June 1988, the Dalai Lama's proposal detailed eleven points addressing Tibetans' fundamental human rights and freedoms, placing the preservation of their cultural and spiritual identity at its core (DIIR 2018(1):227–236; Appendix F). Genuine autonomy would involve a decentralised system enabling Tibetans to engage in self-rule when it comes to domestic affairs, especially religious affairs, while foreign policy and national defence would remain under Beijing's authority (VAN WALT VAN PRAAG/BOLTJES 2020:164). On 21 September 1988, the PRC announced that the proposal would not be taken up for discussion, on the grounds that it does not abandon the concept of Tibet's independence (DIIR 2016:9).

The Dalai Lama's compromise in renouncing independence in favour of autonomy "had no effect on the Chinese authority's willingness to negotiate either" (ROEMER 2010:84). It was still demanded that he agree with the CCP and concede that Tibet had never been independent, so as to give legitimacy to the CCP's actions in Tibet. If the Dalai Lama were to do so, freedoms in Tibet would be restricted even further (ROEMER 2010:84). Despite the setbacks, the CTA reiterates that the past cannot be rewritten: "the distinctive feature of the Middle-Way Policy is that history should not be an obstacle in seeking a mutually beneficial common future within the People's Republic of China." (DIIR 2016:4). Consequently, in 2008, an MWA proposal, the Memorandum on Genuine Autonomy for the Tibetan People, was presented to Beijing within the framework of a dialogue that was resumed in 2002. Focusing on the interests of Tibetans, the Dalai Lama and the CTA specify that no agreement on autonomy will be used "as stepping stone for separation from the PRC." (DIIR 2016:37). Nevertheless, the MWA inspires suspicion on the part of the CCP, which sees it as a devious means for gaining some form of independence for Tibet. Moreover, the Party's distrust of the Dalai Lama and all foreign forces is pervasive (CHINA DAILY 2006). There has been no formal dialogue since January 2010 (Van Walt Van Praag/BOLTJES 2020:168). Despite the many challenges, the MWA remains to this day the central policy of the Dalai Lama and the CTA (VAN WALT VAN PRAAG/BOLTJES 2020:165; CECC 2018:60).

So far, dialogue has failed to gain traction or to bring about concrete actions to address Tibetans' grievances. The situation is unlikely to change with a Chinese government that perceives Tibetan Buddhism and religious figures, such as the Dalai Lama, as threats rather than peacebuilders. Yet, it must be acknowledged that the Dalai Lama has always promoted nonviolence as the only acceptable approach to the Tibet question (ROEMER 2010:83), declaring that he would resign if Tibetans were to violently rebel (CHANGCHING 2015:25). Furthermore, the testimonies underline that if an agreement were to be reached between the CCP and the Dalai Lama, most Tibetans would accept it (Interviews #1, #3, #4, #13; Barnett 2007:10; DIIR 2016:6). A durable peace is therefore unlikely to be reached without the active involvement of religious figures, and especially of the Dalai Lama. With the ongoing human rights violations in Tibet and the introduction of the 2020 National Security Law in Hong Kong, however, it is unlikely that the CCP will update the 17-Point Agreement or grant a "one country, two systems" model to Tibet, so as to address the realities faced by Tibetans. The interviewees are, in fact, less hopeful regarding the MWA and express scepticism about the willingness of the PRC to improve Tibetans' situation. One interviewee admits that asking for autonomy or independence was "not really important, because China doesn't respect anything. They ignore it." (Interview #3). Another interviewee thinks that the MWA could bring positive changes, but admits "there is no choice. Tibet is already burning" (Interview #4). One witness even says "as for me, I don't fully understand the Middle Way. We need to save our cultural heritage, but China refuses both [independence and autonomy]." (Interview #13). "For me," says a former nomad, "I have one dream, it's the return of the Dalai Lama and freedom." He explains that although Tibet's independence should be restored, the MWA would allow Tibetans to have "at least real autonomy to protect our culture, language, identity and our way of thinking." (Interview #12). The interviewees feel that their support for the MWA is more of a default choice in the absence of another opportunity. Indeed, the issue of Tibet has, so far, only been discussed between the elites on both sides. The population has little or no voice in the discussion. Regarding the MWA, even though the initiative was welcomed by exiles, the Tibetan diaspora's approval was not unanimous, as some believed that a decision made in exile might not represent the opinions and needs of Tibetans in Tibet (ROEMER 2010:85).

5.3 Tibetan Resiliency and the Pursuit of Peace

Boss defines resiliency "as the ability to regain one's energy after adversity drains it." (BOSS 2006:27). Such an ability to overcome traumatic events and progress necessitates remarkable resilience (BOSS 2006:47). Tibetan witnesses explain that Buddhist philosophy plays a vital role in developing and strengthening resilience, a competence necessary to limit damage and pain (Interviews #1, #14). Empathy, meditation and a genuine willingness to grow spiritually are essential: "Working on our mind and improving our thinking prevents us from making a difficulty bigger and becoming a more painful problem." (Interview #1). Other interviewees add that Tibetans also draw their strength from their common identity, their patience (Interview #22), their shared struggle and their Buddhist faith and devotion to the Dalai Lama (Interviews #5, #6). Tibetans' resilience is a capacity that is necessary to limit the damage caused by violence in Tibet and to find a peaceful way to deal with it. It could also be considered an act of resistance in itself, by not letting the Chinese oppression defeat Tibetans' spirit. These testimonies show the sense of unity that persists among Tibetans. It gives them the strength to resist, which explains the efforts of the CCP to break it, particularly by interfering in Tibetans' Buddhist way of life.

> *It is a state of war, and if Tibetans were not such dedicated Buddhists, there would be an open conflict. But Tibetans, especially young Tibetans, are feeling increasingly frustrated, and this leads to fears of further major demonstrations and violent responses from the Chinese. (Interview #6)*

> *If you think about the torture that you have suffered from, you make yourself sad. By accepting a situation, you cannot change, you preserve yourself from more suffering that you would inflict on yourself. You have to accept the suffering of existence, or samsara. Tolerance is important. Achieving powerful resilience requires a lot of meditation and study of Buddhist philosophy. (Interview #14)*

> *Patience is instilled from an early age in Tibet. It is a transcendent virtue in Buddhism. But each Tibetan has his or her own way of facing suffering, and of transforming it towards the path to enlightenment. (Interview #22)*

Encouraging interactions between Tibetans and Han Chinese are even more important since the dialogue between the representatives of the two powers, i.e. the CTA and the CCP, has come to a political standstill. Tibetans and Han Chinese do potentially share common interests and values that could be placed in the foreground. Intercultural communication should be promoted. For instance, it is important to recall that Han Chinese Buddhists are reported to comprise 18.2 per cent of the PRC's population (USDOS May 2021). Buddhists, whether Tibetan or Han Chinese, share in the principles of tolerance, self-improvement and by the high value they place on all forms of life espoused by their religion (JONES 1989:263). The Buddhist tradition aims to help believers to cultivate kindness and compassion, in order to drive out negative emotions (or energy), such as hostility and envy. Such practice is the essence of the bodhisattva, "a being who does not disappear into nirvana but watches the universe to protect and assist those who suffer." (NGO/SMYER YU/VAN DER VEER 2015:413). In Mahayana Buddhism, Avalokitesvara is the most esteemed of the bodhisattvas. In Tibet, the Dalai Lama is believed to be his incarnation, while in the PRC, this bodhisattva is also worshipped in the form of a female deity known as Guanyin (NGO/SMYER YU/VAN DER VEER 2015:413). If genuine efforts were made to understand Buddhist traditions, practices and values, and if the presence of Buddhism in both Tibet and the PRC were promoted and empowered, this would represent an asset for peaceful dialogue and positive change. The testimonies underline Tibetans' responsibility to choose nonviolence, rooted in their commitment to self-improvement, a core value in Buddhist teachings. They should be empowered and involved in dialogue as a result of their dedication to inner and world peace, tolerance and reconciliation (NGO/SMYER YU/Van der veer 2015:412). Moreover, compassion and mindfulness lead Buddhists "to look past the immediate intentions of an aggressor to the underlying cause of the violence in question" (APPLEBY 2000: 305–306).

This story is a great example of resilience. An abbot of the Sakya lineage lived in Kham before the occupation. When the Chinese arrived, he was imprisoned for more than 20 years, and was tortured and mistreated. In the 1980s, he managed to go into exile in Nepal, and later became the abbot of a major Buddhist institute in India. He had a good relationship with the Dalai Lama. While in exile, he said that, during his imprisonment:

> *"My greatest suffering, my greatest fear was to lose my compassion and patience for my Chinese torturers."*
> (Interview #22)

> *During and after prison, every day, every hour, what helped me was knowing that the Dalai Lama exists, that he is there. What I did was not a crime. I did not steal or kill. It was for a good cause: standing up for the truth. Buddhist practices also helped a lot, as did secretly reciting prayers when I was in prison.* (Interview #24)

> *Before 2008, resistance was largely rooted in monasteries. After 2008, Tibetans got more involved. Maybe because there was more education and consciousness of the problem.* (Interview #22)

> *Swiss people tend to think we are soft, uncivilised, uneducated. I really hope they will cherish our efforts, for Tibet's sake and for humanity's sake.* (Interview #10)

> *I think that for every Tibetan, the regime is an enemy. It has killed our elders. We can't ignore the past, what they went through, from generation to generation. A strong spirit and patience allow us not to forget. The more Chinese repression there is, the more resistance there will be. We believe a peaceful outcome is possible; this is why Tibetans resist and even sacrifice themselves.* (Interview #23)

Lederach's work promotes communication and mutual understanding as an important part of conflict transformation. The focus is on participative and nonviolent actions aimed at encouraging interactions, dialogue and constructive social change between actors. This approach "includes trying to bring to the surface explicitly the relational fears, hopes, and goals of the people involved" (LEDERACH 2003:24). In the case of Tibet, it also implies launching neutral initiatives that maintain their distance from sensitive issues, in order to avoid exacerbating tensions or attracting attention from security forces. The testimonies showed that the lack of interaction between Tibetans and Han Chinese has allowed discrimination and marginalisation to persist. It also prevents Tibetans from giving voice to their grievances and the violence they experience. The challenge is that interactions between Tibetans and

Han Chinese in Tibet are tightly restricted and remain superficial, notably due to the restrictions of movement imposed by the Chinese authorities, which particularly affects Tibetans in the TAR. The widespread censorship and monitoring of the population affecting both Tibetans and Han Chinese also limits interactions. The influx of information is closely monitored via the mass surveillance of public spaces, as well as police intrusions into private homes and civic institutions, such as monasteries. Consequently, Tibetans refrain from talking to visitors, out of fear of arrest, interrogation and accusations of divulging "state secrets" (Interviews #1, #6, #9, #17, #23).

Nonetheless, far from seeking to isolate Tibet, the interviewees expressed a desire to be able to share their traditions, values, beliefs and stories with the Han Chinese, and to learn more about them in return, without interference from the Chinese authorities. They did not express resentment towards the Han Chinese, but rather towards the misinformation and censorship imposed by the CCP. The needs of Tibetans and Han Chinese are the same, as are the needs of any human being. They strive for certainty about their future, to connect with each other, to contribute to their society and community growth, and to feel significant and safe. Tibetans are entitled to feel humanised. The promotion of mutual respect for social cohesion would benefit both parties and restore the dignity of Tibetans and reintegrate them as equal citizens, opening the way to mutual trust and reconciliation between both the populations and the authorities. One possible common ground based on Buddhism was mentioned above, but a cultural peacebuilding approach seems more relevant and accessible for most Han Chinese. The priority is to discover others on the most neutral ground possible, in order to build trust. If the security situation in Tibet does not allow for advocacy or outreach, or only does so with in difficult or even dangerous circumstances, individual initiatives could be encouraged in the form of development projects. Development initiatives should be culturally sensitive and involve both Tibetans and Han Chinese. These voluntary collaborations would require active and well-informed participation, which would help to create social ties, encourage discussions and lead to greater mutual understanding and empathy. For instance, collaborations between Tibetan nomads and Han Chinese on environmental protection projects should be promoted. Such interactions would also empower nomads, in addition to validating their knowledge and skills in preserving their ecological environment. The restoration of monasteries or historical sites by Tibetan and Han Chinese volunteers could also help to foster these important interactions, as well as reducing discrimination and marginalisation. A more socially responsible form of tourism could also be promoted, one that is more focused on the Tibetan people, in lieu of the red tourism trend in the PRC. To take the example of sky burials, unintrusive educational alternatives should be offered to help inform visitors and to allow them to experience the rite from a distance, in a way that respects local customs. In Tibet, the scope of action is limited and, consequently, the positive outcomes of initiatives enabling genuine interactions, understanding and empathy, may bear fruit over time. Nevertheless, any rapprochement that encourages tolerance is beneficial, regardless of the timeframe.

Conclusion

Tibetans live in a society that is anxiety-provoking for many. Along with the ongoing repression, Tibetans face another form of violence: the lack of official recognition of their struggle by the PRC and the international community, which plunges past atrocities into oblivion. As a result, some Tibetans feel compelled to resort to self-immolation in order to be heard. Nevertheless, Tibetans residing in Tibet and in the diaspora do not want to be victims: "they want to act, to be actors in their future and the peace process in Tibet." (Interview #5). Even after decades of repression, the Tibetans interviewed were genuinely careful to distinguish Chinese citizens from the perpetrators of the exactions ordered by the CCP. Choosing peaceful measures and resilience requires more courage and control of mind and body than violence does. For this reason, their resilience also testifies to their knowledge and experience, as they all aim to improve the situation of Tibetans without the use of force. Yet, if the testimonies show Tibetans' empowering capacity for resilience, their suffering, if not addressed, can be passed on to the next generation.

Two things have never changed though: the night sky that the Himalayas are so close to and the 14th Dalai Lama. (Interview #16)

Potala Palace. *Morel, Lhasa, TAR, 2019.*

CONCLUSION

The rich diversity of cultural expression in the PRC is being buried in silence amidst widespread indifference. Cultural identities lose their *raison d'être* as a result of their becoming a political tool for the CCP, rather than the people's voice. The violations of cultural rights in Tibet represent an assault on Tibetans' right to exist. The use of various forms of violence has become systematic, being deployed to sanction dissidents and independent thinkers, to frighten citizens and to silence witnesses. The interviewees recounted several cases of unnatural deaths, enforced disappearances, arbitrary arrests and lengthy prison sentences. Tibetans continue to be detained by Chinese government representatives without access to fair trials or legal protection. While researching this study, I repeatedly encountered testimonies of acts of torture and other cruel, inhumane or degrading treatments or punishments that represent a recurrent form of violent intimidation used the Chinese authorities. Tibetans are more vulnerable to discrimination, marginalisation and thus to poverty. Silenced by the ongoing repression, some Tibetans go so far as to sacrifice their own lives, hoping that their distress will be heard. However, the CCP does not respond to Tibetans' grievances and needs. It prefers to blame social instability on foreign forces or even to deny that violent events really occurred. The testimonies demonstrated the causal link between violations of cultural rights and the various forms of psychological and physical violence endured by Tibetans, who are significantly harmed in their faith. The testimonies presented in this study show that the methods used by the CCP are proving ineffective in bringing about genuine peace in Tibet. They contribute to the development of feelings of powerlessness and to the loss of the legitimate expression of oneself and needs amongst Tibetans. The respect and protection of cultural diversity are necessary, free from Party interference. The CCP takes little to no account of the human dimension in its management of cultural diversity, exacerbating existing suffering and tensions. By controlling all means of expression of Tibetans' cultural identity, which it sees above all in terms of economic and political affairs, the CCP seeks to break down their sense of common belonging in order to impose its own interpretation of national unity. To this day, the CCP sees Buddhism as a significant political threat and does not promote intercultural communication. Yet, Buddhist leaders, particularly the Dalai Lama, are a significant force for peace and could be valuable mediators between Tibetans and the Chinese government.

Numerous violations of human rights related by witnesses in Chapters 3 and 4 were described in terms of Lemkin's concept of genocide. It was found that several examples of techniques of genocide were, and still are, being deployed in Tibet (LEMKIN 1944:82–90). These violations not only trigger brutalities against civilians; they also contribute to the destruction of their society. The mass killings in Tibet, the famine, the Cultural Revolution and the ongoing repression are responsible for massive human losses and widespread suffering, strengthened by the CCP's regime of fear (LEMKIN 1944:86,88–89). While particular acts of genocide have been recognised (LIC 1960:17), there is as yet no recognition of full genocide in the legal sense. However, as Lemkin points out, genocide does not necessarily lead to the immediate destruction of a community. Its absorption by the dominant state is the result of genocidal techniques, "an elaborate, almost scientific, system" (LEMKIN 1944:90), aiming at the destruction of its essential foundations (LEMKIN 1944:79) and the erasure of its memory. These techniques result in systematic and widespread physical and mental harm, aiming to undermine peoples' psychological stability. Without representing an exhaustive list, several genocidal techniques have been identified in the course of this study. In order to disrupt any sense of unity and weaken the spiritual resistance of Tibetans (LEMKIN 1944:89–90), Buddhism, along with any form of intellectual and cultural expression, is being altered, restricted, banned or even eliminated by the Chinese authorities (LEMKIN 1944:83–84). Tibetans who possess intellectual, moral and spiritual influence are forced into exile, persecuted or killed (LEMKIN 1944:83, 89). Given Buddhism's central role in Tibet, the Party is especially keen to disrupt religious influences and leadership, and above all that of the Dalai Lama, leading it to interfere in the activities of monasteries and the education system (LEMKIN 1944:89). The PRC has replaced local institutions of self-governance with its own representatives and imposed Chinese laws (LEMKIN 1944:82). Its measures and policies have led to a decline in the standard of living of many Tibetans. The CCP took control of the economic structure of Tibet and destroyed the Tibetan economic system, including Tibetans' traditional means of subsistence. By depriving Tibetans of religious freedom, the CCP makes it difficult, if not impossible, for them to fulfil the cultural and spiritual needs necessary to their welfare. By notably restricting or banning their access to monasteries, the Party seeks to divert Tibetans away from moral reflection and to weaken their spiritual resistance (LEMKIN 1944:85, 89–90). In addition, restrictions on movement, coupled with the mass tourism and settlement of Han Chinese in Tibet, reinforce the isolation, marginalisation and multiple forms of discrimination suffered by Tibetans. The latter may enjoy some economic and social benefits if they submit to Chinese rule, but this is not systematic (LEMKIN 1944:85–86). Testimonies have shown that, in particular, the lifestyle choices of nuns, monks and remain dependent on the PRC's whims, despite their compliance. Tibetans' memory and future lie in the hands of the CCP. The measures implemented by the Party mentioned in this work are aimed at moulding Tibetans to the Party's one-track thinking and result in recurrent and widespread violations of human rights. Tibetans have little opportunity to make decisions for themselves and to improve their condition without international support. Taking into account all of these aspects, we can say that crimes against humanity have been committed using genocidal techniques. Moreover, psychological violence in Tibet is alarming. Through their Strike Hard and patriotic re-education campaigns, along with increasingly severe policies and measures restricting every aspect of Tibetans' lives, government officials are accountable for the disappearance of Tibetans' cultural existence, as well as endangering their lives. The inability or unwillingness of the CCP to address grievances and provide protection to Tibetans is a source of serious concern. Lemkin's work allows us to understand the extent and seriousness of culture-based violence in Tibet. This study, while not exhaustive in relation to the extent of the abuses endured by Tibetans, has also highlighted that acts intended to destroy the Tibetan peoples, in whole or in part, as referred by the 1948 Convention on the Prevention and Punishment of the Crime of Genocide, may have been committed in Tibet. These notably include the mass deaths and mass killings of Tibetans and of prominent community or religious leaders (Article 2.a), acts of torture and other cruel, inhuman or degrading treatment or punishment, the intentional infliction of emotional distress (Article 2.b), the infliction of untenable working and economic conditions, notably on nomads, endangering their survival (Article 2.c), and the separation of children from their families to educate them in a Han Chinese environment (Article 2.e). Moreover, in 2020 the PRC continued its policies aimed at effecting demographic change, especially in Tibet, Xinjiang and Inner Mongolia (Article 2.d), "including large-scale resettlement, work-transfer programs, forced sterilizations, and mass internment" (Freedom House 2021). According to sources, the TAR was the testing ground for many of the genocidal techniques used in Xinjiang against the Uyghurs and members of other Muslim minorities (HRW 2018; United States Senate Committee on Foreign Relations 2018). In view of these considerations, the possibility should not be excluded that genocide has been committed in Tibet in the legal sense. Efforts must continue to advocate for human rights in Tibet and the PRC. Tibetans and Tibet, like "every nation", as Lemkin writes, "are essential elements of the world community. [...] The destruction of a nation, therefore, results in the loss of its future contributions to the world. Moreover, such destruction offends our feelings of morality and justice in much the same way as does the criminal killing of a human being [...]." (LEMKIN 1944:91). Raising awareness can help make further atrocities less likely, as well as prevent history from repeating itself during the 2022 Beijing Winter Olympics.

Recommendations

- The PRC must guarantee in all circumstances the physical integrity and psychological well-being of the Tibetan population and must put an end to all acts of harassment

- The PRC must address vulnerabilities and their effect on Tibetans victims of violence, discrimination and marginalisation

- The PRC must also guarantee the rights to freedom of expression, freedom of peaceful assembly, and freedom of association, as enshrined in international human rights law

- The PRC should promote cross-cultural education and socialization without interfering

- Genuine interactions and activities without entering into politicization must be promoted between the Tibetan and Han Chinese populations to create social ties, encourage discussions and lead to greater mutual understanding and empathy.

APPENDICES

Appendix A

Convention on the Prevention and Punishment
of the Crime of Genocide

*Approved and proposed for signature and ratification or accession by
General Assembly resolution 260 A (III) of 9 December 1948
Entry into force: 12 January 1951, in accordance with article XIII*

The Contracting Parties,

Having considered the declaration made by the General Assembly of the United Nations in its resolution 96 (I) dated 11 December 1946 that genocide is a crime under international law, contrary to the spirit and aims of the United Nations and condemned by the civilized world,

Recognizing that at all periods of history genocide has inflicted great losses on humanity, and

Being convinced that, in order to liberate mankind from such an odious scourge, international co-operation is required,

Hereby agree as hereinafter provided:

Article I
The Contracting Parties confirm that genocide, whether committed in time of peace or in time of war, is a crime under international law which they undertake to prevent and to punish.

Article II

In the present Convention, genocide means any of the following acts committed with intent to destroy, in whole or in part, a national, ethnical, racial or religious group, as such:

(a) Killing members of the group;

(b) Causing serious bodily or mental harm to members of the group;

(c) Deliberately inflicting on the group conditions of life calculated to bring about its physical destruction in whole or in part;

(d) Imposing measures intended to prevent births within the group;

(e) Forcibly transferring children of the group to another group.

Article III

The following acts shall be punishable:

(a) Genocide;

(b) Conspiracy to commit genocide;

(c) Direct and public incitement to commit genocide;

(d) Attempt to commit genocide;

(e) Complicity in genocide.

Article IV

Persons committing genocide or any of the other acts enumerated in article III shall be punished, whether they are constitutionally responsible rulers, public officials or private individuals.

Article V

The Contracting Parties undertake to enact, in accordance with their respective Constitutions, the necessary legislation to give effect to the provisions of the present Convention, and, in particular, to provide effective penalties for persons guilty of genocide or any of the other acts enumerated in article III.

Article VI

Persons charged with genocide or any of the other acts enumerated in article III shall be tried by a competent tribunal of the State in the territory of which the act was committed, or by such international penal tribunal as may have jurisdiction with respect to those Contracting Parties which shall have accepted its jurisdiction.

Article VII

Genocide and the other acts enumerated in article III shall not be considered as political crimes for the purpose of extradition.

The Contracting Parties pledge themselves in such cases to grant extradition in accordance with their laws and treaties in force.

Article VIII

Any Contracting Party may call upon the competent organs of the United Nations to take such action under the Charter of the United Nations as they consider appropriate for the prevention and suppression of acts of genocide or any of the other acts enumerated in article III.

Article IX

Disputes between the Contracting Parties relating to the interpretation, application or fulfilment of the present Convention, including those relating to the responsibility of a State for genocide or for any of the other acts enumerated in article III, shall be submitted to the International Court of Justice at the request of any of the parties to the dispute.

Article X

The present Convention, of which the Chinese, English, French, Russian and Spanish texts are equally authentic, shall bear the date of 9 December 1948.

Article XI

The present Convention shall be open until 31 December 1949 for signature on behalf of any Member of the United Nations and of any non-member State to which an invitation to sign has been addressed by the General Assembly.

The present Convention shall be ratified, and the instruments of ratification shall be deposited with the Secretary-General of the United Nations.

After 1 January 1950, the present Convention may be acceded to on behalf of any Member of the United Nations and of any non-member State which has received an invitation as aforesaid.

Instruments of accession shall be deposited with the Secretary-General of the United Nations.

Article XII

Any Contracting Party may at any time, by notification addressed to the Secretary-General of the United Nations, extend the application of the present Convention to all or any of the territories for the conduct of whose foreign relations that Contracting Party is responsible.

Article XIII

On the day when the first twenty instruments of ratification or accession have been deposited, the Secretary-General shall draw up a procès-verbal and transmit a copy thereof to each Member of the United Nations and to each of the non-member States contemplated in article XI.

The present Convention shall come into force on the ninetieth day following the date of deposit of the twentieth instrument of ratification or accession.

Any ratification or accession effected subsequent to the latter date shall become effective on the ninetieth day following the deposit of the instrument of ratification or accession.

Article XIV

The present Convention shall remain in effect for a period of ten years as from the date of its coming into force.

It shall thereafter remain in force for successive periods of five years for such Contracting Parties as have not denounced it at least six months before the expiration of the current period.

Denunciation shall be effected by a written notification addressed to the Secretary-General of the United Nations.

Article XV

If, as a result of denunciations, the number of Parties to the present Convention should become less than sixteen, the Convention shall cease to be in force as from the date on which the last of these denunciations shall become effective.

Article XVI

A request for the revision of the present Convention may be made at any time by any Contracting Party by means of a notification in writing addressed to the Secretary-General.

The General Assembly shall decide upon the steps, if any, to be taken in respect of such request.

Article XVII

The Secretary-General of the United Nations shall notify all Members of the United Nations and the non-member States contemplated in article XI of the following:

(a) Signatures, ratifications and accessions received in accordance with article XI;

(b) Notifications received in accordance with article XII;

(c) The date upon which the present Convention comes into force in accordance with article XIII;

(d) Denunciations received in accordance with article XIV;

(e) The abrogation of the Convention in accordance with article XV;

(f) Notifications received in accordance with article XVI.

Article XVIII

The original of the present Convention shall be deposited in the archives of the United Nations.

A certified copy of the Convention shall be transmitted to each Member of the United Nations and to each of the non-member States contemplated in article XI.

Article XIX

The present Convention shall be registered by the Secretary-General of the United Nations on the date of its coming into force.

Appendix B

United Nations Declaration on the Rights of Indigenous Peoples
Resolution adopted by the General Assembly

[without reference to a Main Committee (A/61/L.67 and Add.1)]

61/295. United Nations Declaration on the Rights of Indigenous Peoples

The General Assembly,

Taking note of the recommendation of the Human Rights Council contained in its resolution 1/2 of 29 June 2006, by which the Council adopted the text of the United Nations Declaration on the Rights of Indigenous Peoples,

Recalling its resolution 61/178 of 20 December 2006, by which it decided to defer consideration of and action on the Declaration to allow time for further consultations thereon, and also decided to conclude its consideration before the end of the sixty-first session of the General Assembly,

Adopts the United Nations Declaration on the Rights of Indigenous Peoples as contained in the annex to the present resolution.

107th plenary meeting

13 September 2007

Annex

United Nations Declaration on the Rights of Indigenous Peoples

The General Assembly,

Guided by the purposes and principles of the Charter of the United Nations, and good faith in the fulfilment of the obligations assumed by States in accordance with the Charter,

Affirming that indigenous peoples are equal to all other peoples, while recognizing the right of all peoples to be different, to consider themselves different, and to be respected as such,

Affirming also that all peoples contribute to the diversity and richness of civilizations and cultures, which constitute the common heritage of humankind,

Affirming further that all doctrines, policies and practices based on or advocating superiority of peoples or individuals on the basis of national origin or racial, religious, ethnic or cultural differences are racist, scientifically false, legally invalid, morally condemnable and socially unjust,

Reaffirming that indigenous peoples, in the exercise of their rights, should be free from discrimination of any kind,

Concerned that indigenous peoples have suffered from historic injustices as a result of, inter alia, their colonization and dispossession of their lands, territories and resources, thus preventing them from exercising, in particular, their right to development in accordance with their own needs and interests,

Recognizing the urgent need to respect and promote the inherent rights of indigenous peoples which derive from their political, economic and social structures and from their cultures, spiritual traditions, histories and philosophies, especially their rights to their lands, territories and resources,

Recognizing also the urgent need to respect and promote the rights of indigenous peoples affirmed in treaties, agreements and other constructive arrangements with States,

Welcoming the fact that indigenous peoples are organizing themselves for political, economic, social and cultural enhancement and in order to bring to an end all forms of discrimination and oppression wherever they occur,

Convinced that control by indigenous peoples over developments affecting them and their lands, territories and resources will enable them to maintain and strengthen their institutions, cultures and traditions, and to promote their development in accordance with their aspirations and needs,

Recognizing that respect for indigenous knowledge, cultures and traditional practices contributes to sustainable and equitable development and proper management of the environment, Emphasizing the contribution of the demilitarization of the lands and territories of indigenous peoples to peace, economic and social progress and development, understanding and friendly relations among nations and peoples of the world,

Recognizing in particular the right of indigenous families and communities to retain shared responsibility for the upbringing, training, education and well-being of their children, consistent with the rights of the child,

Considering that the rights affirmed in treaties, agreements and other constructive arrangements between States and indigenous peoples are, in some situations, matters of international concern, interest, responsibility and character,

Considering also that treaties, agreements and other constructive arrangements, and the relationship they represent, are the basis for a strengthened partnership between indigenous peoples and States,

Acknowledging that the Charter of the United Nations, the International Covenant on Economic, Social and Cultural Rights and the International Covenant on Civil and Political Rights,[2] as well as the Vienna Declaration and Programme of Action, affirm the fundamental importance of the right to self-determination of all peoples, by virtue of which they freely determine their political status and freely pursue their economic, social and cultural development,

Bearing in mind that nothing in this Declaration may be used to deny any peoples their right to self-determination, exercised in conformity with international law,

Convinced that the recognition of the rights of indigenous peoples in this Declaration will enhance harmonious and cooperative relations between the State and indigenous peoples, based on principles of justice, democracy, respect for human rights, non-discrimination and good faith,

Encouraging States to comply with and effectively implement all their obligations as they apply to indigenous peoples under international instruments, in particular those related to human rights, in consultation and cooperation with the peoples concerned,

Emphasizing that the United Nations has an important and continuing role to play in promoting and protecting the rights of indigenous peoples,

Believing that this Declaration is a further important step forward for the recognition, promotion and protection of the rights and freedoms of indigenous peoples and in the development of relevant activities of the United Nations system in this field,

Recognizing and reaffirming that indigenous individuals are entitled without discrimination to all human rights recognized in international law, and that indigenous peoples possess collective rights which are indispensable for their existence, well-being and integral development as peoples,

Recognizing that the situation of indigenous peoples varies from region to region and from country to country and that the significance of national and regional particularities and various historical and cultural backgrounds should be taken into consideration,

Solemnly proclaims the following United Nations Declaration on the Rights of Indigenous Peoples as a standard of achievement to be pursued in a spirit of partnership and mutual respect:

Article 1

Indigenous peoples have the right to the full enjoyment, as a collective or as individuals, of all human rights and fundamental freedoms as recognized in the Charter of the United Nations, the Universal Declaration of Human Rights and international human rights law.

Article 2

Indigenous peoples and individuals are free and equal to all other peoples and individuals and have the right to be free from any kind of discrimination, in the exercise of their rights, in particular that based on their indigenous origin or identity.

Article 3

Indigenous peoples have the right to self-determination. By virtue of that right they freely determine their political status and freely pursue their economic, social and cultural development.

Article 4

Indigenous peoples, in exercising their right to self-determination, have the right to autonomy or self-government in matters relating to their internal and local affairs, as well as ways and means for financing their autonomous functions.

Article 5

Indigenous peoples have the right to maintain and strengthen their distinct political, legal, economic, social and cultural institutions, while retaining their right to participate fully, if they so choose, in the political, economic, social and cultural life of the State.

Article 6

Every indigenous individual has the right to a nationality.

Article 7

1. Indigenous individuals have the rights to life, physical and mental integrity, liberty and security of person.

2. Indigenous peoples have the collective right to live in freedom, peace and security as distinct peoples and shall not be subjected to any act of genocide or any other act of violence, including forcibly removing children of the group to another group.

Article 8

1. Indigenous peoples and individuals have the right not to be subjected to forced assimilation or destruction of their culture.

2. States shall provide effective mechanisms for prevention of, and redress for:

> (a) Any action which has the aim or effect of depriving them of their integrity as distinct peoples, or of their cultural values or ethnic identities;
>
> (b) Any action which has the aim or effect of dispossessing them of their lands, territories or resources;
>
> (c) Any form of forced population transfer which has the aim or effect of violating or undermining any of their rights;
>
> (d) Any form of forced assimilation or integration;
>
> (e) Any form of propaganda designed to promote or incite racial or ethnic discrimination directed against them.

Article 9

Indigenous peoples and individuals have the right to belong to an indigenous community or nation, in accordance with the traditions and customs of the community or nation concerned. No discrimination of any kind may arise from the exercise of such a right.

Article 10

Indigenous peoples shall not be forcibly removed from their lands or territories. No relocation shall take place without the free, prior and informed consent of the indigenous peoples concerned and after agreement on just and fair compensation and, where possible, with the option of return.

Article 11

1. Indigenous peoples have the right to practise and revitalize their cultural traditions and customs. This includes the right to maintain, protect and develop the past, present and future manifestations of their cultures, such as archaeological and historical sites, artefacts, designs, ceremonies, technologies and visual and performing arts and literature.

2. States shall provide redress through effective mechanisms, which may include restitution, developed in conjunction with indigenous peoples, with respect to their cultural, intellectual, religious and spiritual property taken without their free, prior and informed consent or in violation of their laws, traditions and customs.

Article 12

1. Indigenous peoples have the right to manifest, practise, develop and teach their spiritual and religious traditions, customs and ceremonies; the right to maintain, protect, and have access in privacy to their religious and cultural sites; the right to the use and control of their ceremonial objects; and the right to the repatriation of their human remains.

2. States shall seek to enable the access and/or repatriation of ceremonial objects and human remains in their possession through fair, transparent and effective mechanisms developed in conjunction with indigenous peoples concerned.

Article 13

1. Indigenous peoples have the right to revitalize, use, develop and transmit to future generations their histories, languages, oral traditions, philosophies, writing systems and literatures, and to designate and retain their own names for communities, places and persons.

2. States shall take effective measures to ensure that this right is protected and also to ensure that indigenous peoples can understand and be understood in political, legal and administrative proceedings, where necessary through the provision of interpretation or by other appropriate means.

Article 14

1. Indigenous peoples have the right to establish and control their educational systems and institutions providing education in their own languages, in a manner appropriate to their cultural methods of teaching and learning.

2. Indigenous individuals, particularly children, have the right to all levels and forms of education of the State without discrimination.

3. States shall, in conjunction with indigenous peoples, take effective measures, in order for indigenous individuals, particularly children, including those living outside their communities, to have access, when possible, to an education in their own culture and provided in their own language.

Article 15

1. Indigenous peoples have the right to the dignity and diversity of their cultures, traditions, histories and aspirations which shall be appropriately reflected in education and public information.

2. States shall take effective measures, in consultation and cooperation with the indigenous peoples concerned, to combat prejudice and eliminate discrimination and to promote tolerance, understanding and good relations among indigenous peoples and all other segments of society.

Article 16

1. Indigenous peoples have the right to establish their own media in their own languages and to have access to all forms of non-indigenous media without discrimination.

2. States shall take effective measures to ensure that State-owned media duly reflect indigenous cultural diversity. States, without prejudice to ensuring full freedom of expression, should encourage privately owned media to adequately reflect indigenous cultural diversity.

Article 17

1. Indigenous individuals and peoples have the right to enjoy fully all rights established under applicable international and domestic labour law.

2. States shall in consultation and cooperation with indigenous peoples take specific measures to protect indigenous children from economic exploitation and from performing any work that is likely to be hazardous or to interfere with the child's education, or to be harmful to the child's health or physical, mental, spiritual, moral or social development, taking into account their special vulnerability and the importance of education for their empowerment.

3. Indigenous individuals have the right not to be subjected to any discriminatory conditions of labour and, inter alia, employment or salary.

Article 18

Indigenous peoples have the right to participate in decision-making in matters which would affect their rights, through representatives chosen by themselves in accordance with their own procedures, as well as to maintain and develop their own indigenous decision-making institutions.

Article 19

States shall consult and cooperate in good faith with the indigenous peoples concerned through their own representative institutions in order to obtain their free, prior and informed consent before adopting and implementing legislative or administrative measures that may affect them.

Article 20

1. Indigenous peoples have the right to maintain and develop their political, economic and social systems or institutions, to be secure in the enjoyment of their own means of subsistence and development, and to engage freely in all their traditional and other economic activities.

2. Indigenous peoples deprived of their means of subsistence and development are entitled to just and fair redress.

Article 21

1. Indigenous peoples have the right, without discrimination, to the improvement of their economic and social conditions, including, inter alia, in the areas of education, employment, vocational training and retraining, housing, sanitation, health and social security.

2. States shall take effective measures and, where appropriate, special measures to ensure continuing improvement of their economic and social conditions. Particular attention shall be paid to the rights and

special needs of indigenous elders, women, youth, children and persons with disabilities.

Article 22

1. Particular attention shall be paid to the rights and special needs of indigenous elders, women, youth, children and persons with disabilities in the implementation of this Declaration.

2. States shall take measures, in conjunction with indigenous peoples, to ensure that indigenous women and children enjoy the full protection and guarantees against all forms of violence and discrimination.

Article 23

Indigenous peoples have the right to determine and develop priorities and strategies for exercising their right to development. In particular, indigenous peoples have the right to be actively involved in developing and determining health, housing and other economic and social programmes affecting them and, as far as possible, to administer such programmes through their own institutions.

Article 24

1. Indigenous peoples have the right to their traditional medicines and to maintain their health practices, including the conservation of their vital medicinal plants, animals and minerals. Indigenous individuals also have the right to access, without any discrimination, to all social and health services.

2. Indigenous individuals have an equal right to the enjoyment of the highest attainable standard of physical and mental health. States shall take the necessary steps with a view to achieving progressively the full realization of this right.

Article 25

Indigenous peoples have the right to maintain and strengthen their distinctive spiritual relationship with their traditionally owned or otherwise occupied and used lands, territories, waters and coastal seas and other resources and to uphold their responsibilities to future generations in this regard.

Article 26

1. Indigenous peoples have the right to the lands, territories and resources which they have traditionally owned, occupied or otherwise used or acquired.

2. Indigenous peoples have the right to own, use, develop and control the lands, territories and resources that they possess by reason of traditional ownership or other traditional occupation or use, as well as those which they have otherwise acquired.

3. States shall give legal recognition and protection to these lands, territories and resources. Such recognition shall be conducted with due respect to the customs, traditions and land tenure systems of the indigenous peoples concerned.

Article 27

States shall establish and implement, in conjunction with indigenous peoples concerned, a fair, independent, impartial, open and transparent process, giving due recognition to indigenous peoples' laws, traditions, customs and land tenure systems, to recognize and adjudicate the rights of indigenous peoples pertaining to their lands, territories and resources, including those which were traditionally owned or otherwise occupied or used. Indigenous peoples shall have the right to participate in this process.

Article 28

1. Indigenous peoples have the right to redress, by means that can include restitution or, when this is not possible, just, fair and equitable compensation, for the lands, territories and resources which they have traditionally owned or otherwise occupied or used, and which have been

confiscated, taken, occupied, used or damaged without their free, prior and informed consent.

2. Unless otherwise freely agreed upon by the peoples concerned, compensation shall take the form of lands, territories and resources equal in quality, size and legal status or of monetary compensation or other appropriate redress.

Article 29

1. Indigenous peoples have the right to the conservation and protection of the environment and the productive capacity of their lands or territories and resources. States shall establish and implement assistance programmes for indigenous peoples for such conservation and protection, without discrimination.

2. States shall take effective measures to ensure that no storage or disposal of hazardous materials shall take place in the lands or territories of indigenous peoples without their free, prior and informed consent.

3. States shall also take effective measures to ensure, as needed, that programmes for monitoring, maintaining and restoring the health of indigenous peoples, as developed and implemented by the peoples affected by such materials, are duly implemented.

Article 30

1. Military activities shall not take place in the lands or territories of indigenous peoples, unless justified by a relevant public interest or otherwise freely agreed with or requested by the indigenous peoples concerned.

2. States shall undertake effective consultations with the indigenous peoples concerned, through appropriate procedures and in particular through their representative institutions, prior to using their lands or territories for military activities.

Article 31

1. Indigenous peoples have the right to maintain, control, protect and develop their cultural heritage, traditional knowledge and traditional cultural expressions, as well as the manifestations of their sciences, technologies and cultures, including human and genetic resources, seeds, medicines, knowledge of the properties of fauna and flora, oral traditions, literatures, designs, sports and traditional games and visual and performing arts. They also have the right to maintain, control, protect and develop their intellectual property over such cultural heritage, traditional knowledge, and traditional cultural expressions.

2. In conjunction with indigenous peoples, States shall take effective measures to recognize and protect the exercise of these rights.

Article 32

1. Indigenous peoples have the right to determine and develop priorities and strategies for the development or use of their lands or territories and other resources.

2. States shall consult and cooperate in good faith with the indigenous peoples concerned through their own representative institutions in order to obtain their free and informed consent prior to the approval of any project affecting their lands or territories and other resources, particularly in connection with the development, utilization or exploitation of mineral, water or other resources.

3. States shall provide effective mechanisms for just and fair redress for any such activities, and appropriate measures shall be taken to mitigate adverse environmental, economic, social, cultural or spiritual impact.

Article 33

1. Indigenous peoples have the right to determine their own identity or membership in accordance with their customs and traditions. This

does not impair the right of indigenous individuals to obtain citizenship of the States in which they live.

2. Indigenous peoples have the right to determine the structures and to select the membership of their institutions in accordance with their own procedures.

Article 34

Indigenous peoples have the right to promote, develop and maintain their institutional structures and their distinctive customs, spirituality, traditions, procedures, practices and, in the cases where they exist, juridical systems or customs, in accordance with international human rights standards.

Article 35

Indigenous peoples have the right to determine the responsibilities of individuals to their communities.

Article 36

1. Indigenous peoples, in particular those divided by international borders, have the right to maintain and develop contacts, relations and cooperation, including activities for spiritual, cultural, political, economic and social purposes, with their own members as well as other peoples across borders.

2. States, in consultation and cooperation with indigenous peoples, shall take effective measures to facilitate the exercise and ensure the implementation of this right.

Article 37

1. Indigenous peoples have the right to the recognition, observance and enforcement of treaties, agreements and other constructive arrangements concluded with States or their successors and to have States honour and respect such treaties, agreements and other constructive arrangements.

2. Nothing in this Declaration may be interpreted as diminishing or eliminating the rights of indigenous peoples contained in treaties, agreements and other constructive arrangements.

Article 38

States, in consultation and cooperation with indigenous peoples, shall take the appropriate measures, including legislative measures, to achieve the ends of this Declaration.

Article 39

Indigenous peoples have the right to have access to financial and technical assistance from States and through international cooperation, for the enjoyment of the rights contained in this Declaration.

Article 40

Indigenous peoples have the right to access to and prompt decision through just and fair procedures for the resolution of conflicts and disputes with States or other parties, as well as to effective remedies for all infringements of their individual and collective rights. Such a decision shall give due consideration to the customs, traditions, rules and legal systems of the indigenous peoples concerned and international human rights.

Article 41

The organs and specialized agencies of the United Nations system and other intergovernmental organizations shall contribute to the full realization of the provisions of this Declaration through the mobilization, inter alia, of financial cooperation and technical assistance. Ways and means of ensuring participation of indigenous peoples on issues affecting them shall be established.

Article 42

The United Nations, its bodies, including the Permanent Forum on Indigenous Issues, and specialized agencies, including at the country level, and States shall promote respect for and full application of the provisions of this Declaration and follow up the effectiveness of this Declaration.

Article 43

The rights recognized herein constitute the minimum standards for the survival, dignity and well-being of the indigenous peoples of the world.

Article 44

All the rights and freedoms recognized herein are equally guaranteed to male and female indigenous individuals.

Article 45

Nothing in this Declaration may be construed as diminishing or extinguishing the rights indigenous peoples have now or may acquire in the future.

Article 46

1. Nothing in this Declaration may be interpreted as implying for any State, people, group or person any right to engage in any activity or to perform any act contrary to the Charter of the United Nations or construed as authorizing or encouraging any action which would dismember or impair, totally or in part, the territorial integrity or political unity of sovereign and independent States.

2. In the exercise of the rights enunciated in the present Declaration, human rights and fundamental freedoms of all shall be respected. The exercise of the rights set forth in this Declaration shall be subject only to such limitations as are determined by law and in accordance with international human rights obligations. Any such limitations shall be non-discriminatory and strictly necessary solely for the purpose of securing due recognition and respect for the rights and freedoms of others and for

meeting the just and most compelling requirements of a democratic society.

3. The provisions set forth in this Declaration shall be interpreted in accordance with the principles of justice, democracy, respect for human rights, equality, non-discrimination, good governance and good faith.

Appendix C

Fribourg Declaration

Issues	Justifications
1 *Fundamental principles* **2** *Definitions*	Principles and definitions
3 *Identity and cultural heritage* **4** *Reference to cultural communities* **5** *Access to and participation in cultural life* **6** *Education and training* **7** *Information and communication* **8** *Cultural cooperation*	Cultural Rights
9 *Principles of democratic governance* **10** *Insertion within the economy* **11** *Responsibility of actors in the public sector* **12** *Responsibility of international organizations*	Implementation

Fribourg Declaration

Recalling the Universal Declaration of Human Rights, the two International Covenants on human rights of the United Nations, the UNESCO Universal Declaration on Cultural Diversity and other relevant universal and regional instruments;

Reaffirming that human rights are universal, indivisible and interdependent and that cultural rights, as much as other human rights, are an expression of and a prerequisite for   human dignity;

Convinced that violations of cultural rights give rise to identity related tensions and conflicts which are one of the principal cause of violence, wars and terrorism;

Equally convinced that cultural diversity cannot be truly protected without the effective implementation of cultural rights;

Considering the need to take into account the cultural dimension of all human rights as recognized today;

Considering also that respect for diversity and cultural rights is a crucial factor in the legitimacy and consistency of sustainable development based upon the indivisibility of human rights;

Observing that cultural rights have been asserted primarily in the context of the rights of minorities and indigenous peoples and that it is essential to guarantee these rights in a universal manner, notably for the most destitute;

Considering that a clarification of the position of cultural rights within the human rights system, as well as a better understanding of their nature and the consequences of violations of these rights constitute the best means to prevent them from being used in support of cultural relativism and that they do not become a pretext for pitting communities or peoples against one another;

Considering also that cultural rights, as expressed in the present Declaration, are currently   recognized in a dispersed manner in a large number of human rights instruments and that it is important to assemble these rights together in order to ensure their visibility and coherence and to encourage their full realisation;

We present this Declaration on cultural rights to actors in the three sectors: public (States and their institutions), civil society (non-governmental organizations and other non-profit associations and institutions) and private (enterprises) with a view to encouraging the recognition and implementation of cultural rights at the local, national, regional and universal levels.

Article 1 *(fundamental principles)*

The rights enunciated in the present Declaration are essential to human dignity. For this reason, they form an integral part of human rights and must be interpreted according to the principles of universality, indivisibility and interdependence. Therefore:

a. These rights are guaranteed without discrimination of any kind such as colour, sex, age, language, religion, conviction, descent, national or ethnic origin, social origin or status, birth or any other situation on the basis of which a person constructs one's cultural identity;

b. No one shall suffer or be discriminated against in any way as a consequence of the exercise or non-exercise of the rights set forth in the present Declaration;

c. No one shall invoke these rights to impair another right recognised in the Universal Declaration or in other human rights instruments;

d. The exercise of cultural rights shall only be subjected to those limitations provided for in international human rights instruments. Nothing in the present Declaration shall affect any provisions which are more conducive to the realisation of cultural rights and which may be contained in national legislation or practice or in international law;

e. The effective realisation of a human right requires that its cultural dimensions are taken into account in light of the fundamental principles enumerated above.

Article 2 *(definitions)*

For the purposes of the present Declaration,

a. The term "culture" covers those values, beliefs, convictions, languages, knowledge and the arts, traditions, institutions and ways of life through which a person or a group expresses their humanity and the meanings that they give to their existence and to their development;

b. The expression "cultural identity" is understood as the sum of all cultural references through which a person, alone or in community with others, defines or constitutes oneself, communicates and wishes to be recognised in one's dignity;

c. "Cultural community" connotes a group of persons who share references that constitute a common cultural identity that they intend to preserve and develop.

Article 3 *(identity and cultural heritage)*

Everyone, alone or in community with others, has the right:

a. To choose and to have one's cultural identity respected, in the variety of its different means of expression. This right is exercised in the inter-connection with, in particular, the freedoms of thought, conscience, religion, opinion and expression;

b. To know and to have one's own culture respected as well as those cultures that, in their diversity, make up the common heritage of humanity. This implies in particular the right to knowledge about human rights and fundamental freedoms, as these are values essential to this heritage;

c. To access, notably through the enjoyment of the rights to education and information, cultural heritages that constitute the expression of different cultures as well as resources for both present and future generations.

Article 4 *(reference to cultural communities)*

a. Everyone is free to choose to identify or not to identify with one or several cultural communities, regardless of frontiers, and to modify such a choice;

b. No one shall have a cultural identity imposed or be assimilated into a cultural community against one's will.

Article 5 *(access to and participation in cultural life)*

a. Everyone, alone or in community with others, has the right to access and participate freely in cultural life through the activities of one's choice, regardless of frontiers.

b. This right includes in particular:

- The freedom to express oneself, in public or in private in the language(s) of one's choice;

- The freedom to exercise, in conformity with the rights recognised in the present Declaration, one's own cultural practices and to follow a way of life associated with the promotion of one's cultural resources, notably in the area of the use of and in the production of goods and services;

- The freedom to develop and share knowledge and cultural expressions, to conduct research and to participate in different forms of creation as well as to benefit from these;

- The right to the protection of the moral and material interests linked to the works that result from one's cultural activity.

Article 6 *(education and training)*

Within the general framework of the right to education, everyone has the right throughout one' lifespan, alone or in community with others, to education and training that, responding to fundamental educational needs, contribute to the free and full development of one's cultural identity while respecting the rights of others and cultural diversity. This right includes in particular:

a. Human rights education and knowledge;

b. The freedom to teach and to receive teaching of and in one's language and in other languages, as well as knowledge related to one's own culture and other cultures;

c. The freedom of parents to ensure the religious and moral education of their children in conformity with their own convictions while respecting the freedom of thought, conscience and religion of the child on the basis of her/his capacities;

d. The freedom to establish, to direct and to have access to educational institutions other than those run by the public authorities, on the condition that the internationally-recognised norms and principles in the area of education are respected and that these institutions conform to the minimum rules prescribed by the State.

Article 7 *(communication and information)*

Within the general framework of the rights to freedom of expression, including artistic freedom, as well as freedom of opinion and information, and with respect for cultural diversity, everyone, alone or in community with others, has the right to free and pluralistic information that contributes to the full development of one's cultural identity. This right, which may be exercised regardless of frontiers, comprises in particular:

    a.   The freedom to seek, receive and impart information;

    b.   The right to participate in pluralist information, in the language(s) of one's choice, to contribute to its production or its dissemination by way of all information and communication technologies;

    c.   The right to respond to erroneous information concerning cultures, with full respect of the rights expressed in this Declaration.

Article 8 *(cultural cooperation)*

Everyone, alone or in community with others, has the right to participate, according to democratic procedures:

- in the cultural development of the communities of which one is a member;

- in the elaboration, implementation and evaluation of decisions that concern oneself and which have an impact on the exercise of one's cultural rights;

- in the development of cultural cooperation at different levels.

Article 9 *(principles of democratic governance)*

The respect, protection and fulfilment of the rights expressed in the present Declaration imply obligations for each person and community. Cultural actors in the three different sectors – public, private and civil – have a particular responsibility within the framework of democratic governance to interact and, if need be, to take initiatives for the purpose of:

a. Ensuring respect for cultural rights and developing means of consultation and participation in order to guarantee their realisation, in particular for those who are most disadvantaged by virtue of their social status or the fact that they belong to a minority;

b. Guaranteeing in particular the interactive exercise of the right to adequate information to ensure that cultural rights are taken into consideration by all actors in the social, economic and political spheres;

c. Train their personnel and raise public awareness on the understanding and respect for all human rights and cultural rights in particular;

d. Identifying and taking into account the cultural dimensions of all human rights in order to enhance universality through diversity and to encourage the appropriation of these rights by all persons, alone or in community with others.

Article 10 *(insertion into the economy)*

Actors in the public, private and civil sectors must, within the framework of their specific mandates and responsibilities:

a. Ensure that the cultural goods and services that carry value, identity and meaning, as well as all other goods to the extent that they have a significant influence on ways of life and other cultural expressions, are conceived, produced and used in a manner that does not impair the rights expressed in the present Declaration;

b. Consider that the cultural compatibility of goods and services is often of crucial importance for persons in disadvantaged situations as a result of poverty, isolation or one's belonging to a discriminated group.

Article 11 *(responsibility of actors in the public sector)*

States and other actors in the public sector must, within the framework of their specific mandates and responsibilities:

a. Incorporate the rights recognized in the present Declaration into their national legislation and practice;

b. Respect, protect and fulfil the rights enunciated in the present Declaration in conditions of equality and dedicate the maximum amount of their available resources to ensure their full exercise;

c. Ensure that anyone who, alone or in community with others, claims that one's cultural rights have been violated, has access to effective remedies, in particular, judicial remedies;

d. Strengthen the means of international cooperation necessary for this implementation, in particular by intensifying their interaction within the relevant international organizations.

Article 12 *(responsibility of international organisations)*

International organisations must, within the framework of their specific mandates and responsibilities:

a. Guarantee that cultural rights and the cultural dimension of other human rights are systematically taken into consideration in all of their activities;

b. Ensure that cultural rights are consistently and progressively integrated into all relevant instruments and monitoring mechanisms;

c. Contribute to the development of common transparent and effective mechanisms for evaluation and monitoring.

Adopted in Fribourg on May 7th 2007

Appendix D

17-Point Agreement

The Agreement of the Central People's Government and the Local Government of Tibet on Measures for the Peaceful Liberation of Tibet

The Tibetan ethnic group is one of the ethnic groups with a long history within the boundaries of China and, like many other ethnic groups, it has performed its glorious duty in the course of the creation and development of our great motherland. But over the last 100 years or more, imperialist forces penetrated into China, and in consequence also penetrated into the Tibetan region and carried out all kinds of deceptions and provocations. Like previous reactionary governments, the Kuomintang reactionary government continued to carry out a policy of oppressing and sowing dissension among the ethnic groups, causing division and disunity among the Tibetan people. And the local government of Tibet did not oppose the imperialist deceptions and provocations, and adopted an unpatriotic attitude towards our great motherland. Under such conditions, the Tibetan ethnic group and people were plunged into the depths of enslavement and suffering.

In 1949, basic victory was achieved on a nationwide scale in the Chinese People's War of Liberation; the common domestic enemy of all ethnic groups—the Kuomintang reactionary government—was overthrown; and the common foreign enemy of all the ethnic groups--the aggressive imperialist forces—was driven out. On this basis, the founding of the People's Republic of China and of the Central People's Government was announced. In accordance with the Common Program passed by the Chinese People's Political Consultative Conference (CPPCC), the Central people's Government declared that all ethnic groups within the boundaries of the People's Republic of China are equal, and that they shall establish unity and mutual aid and oppose imperialism and their own public enemies, so that the People's Republic of China will become a big fraternal and cooperative family, composed of all its ethnic groups; that within the big family of all ethnic groups of the People's Republic of China, national regional autonomy shall be exercised in areas where national minorities are concentrated, and all national minorities shall have freedom to develop their spoken and written languages and to preserve or People's Government shall assist all ethnic minorities to develop their political, economic, cultural and educational construction work. Since then, all ethnic groups within the country, with the exception of those in the areas of Tibet and Taiwan, have gained liberation. Under the unified leadership of the Central People's Government and the direct leadership of higher levels of People's Governments, all ethnic minorities are full enjoying the right of national equality and have established, or are establishing, national regional autonomy.

In order that the influences of aggressive imperialist forces in Tibet might be successfully eliminated, the unification of the territory and sovereignty of the People's Republic of China accomplished, and national defense safeguarded; in order that the Tibetan ethnic group and people might be freed and return to the big family of the People's Republic of China to enjoy the same rights of national equality as all the other ethnic groups in the country and develop their political, economic, cultural and educational work, the Central People's Government, when it ordered the People's Liberation Army to march into Tibet, notified the local government of Tibet to send delegates to the central authorities to conduct talks for the conclusion of an agreement on measures for the peaceful liberation of Tibet.

In the latter part of April 1951, the delegates with full powers of the local government of Tibet arrived in Beijing. The Central People's Government appointed representatives with full powers to conduct talks on a friendly basis with the delegates with full powers of the local government of Tibet. As a result of these talks, both parties agreed to conclude this agreement and guarantee that it will be carried into effect.

1. The Tibetan people shall unite and drive out imperialist aggressive forces from Tibet; the Tibetan people shall return to the big family of the motherland—the People's Republic of China.

2. The local government of Tibet shall actively assist the People's Liberation Army to enter Tibet and consolidate the national defense.

3. In accordance with the policy towards ethnic groups laid down in the Common Program of the CPPCC [Chinese People's Political Consultative Conference], the Tibetan people have the right of exercising national regional autonomy under the unified leadership of the Central People's Government.

4. The central authorities will not alter the existing political system in Tibet. The central authorities also will not alter the established status, functions and powers of the Dalai Lama. Officials of various ranks shall hold office as usual.

5. The established status, functions and powers of the Panchen Erdeni [Panchen Lama] shall be maintained.

6. By the established status, functions and powers of the Dalai Lama and of the Panchen Erdeni are meant the status, functions and powers of the 13th Dalai Lama and of the 9th Panchen Erdeni when they were in friendly and amicable relations with each other.

7. The policy of freedom of religious belief laid down in the Common Program of the CPPCC shall be carried out. The religious beliefs, customs and habits of the Tibetan people shall be respected, and lama-monasteries shall be protected. The central authorities will not effect a change in the income of the monasteries.

8. Tibetan troops shall be reorganized by stages into the People's Liberation Army, and become a part of the national defense forces of the People's Republic of China.

9. The spoken and written language and school education of the Tibetan ethnic group shall be developed step by step in accordance with the actual conditions in Tibet.

10. Tibetan agriculture, livestock raising, industry and commerce shall be developed step by step, and the people's livelihood shall be improved step by step in accordance with the actual conditions in Tibet.

11. In matters related to various reforms in Tibet, there will be no compulsion on the part of the central authorities. The local government of Tibet should carry out reforms of its own accord, and when the people raise demands for reform, they shall be settled by means of consultation with the leading personnel of Tibet.

12. In so far as former pro-imperialist and pro-Kuomintang officials resolutely sever relations with imperialism and the Kuomintang and do not engage in sabotage or resistance, they may continue to hold office irrespective of their past.

13. The People's Liberation Army entering Tibet shall abide by all the above-mentioned policies and shall also be fair in all buying and selling and shall not arbitrarily take a single needle or thread from the people.

14. The Central People's Government shall conduct the centralized handling of all external affairs of the area of Tibet; and there will be peaceful co-existence with neighboring countries and establishment and development of fair commercial and trading relations with them on the basis of equality, mutual benefit and mutual respect for territory and sovereignty.

15. In order to ensure the implementation of this agreement, the Central People's Government shall set up a military and administrative committee and a military area   headquarters in Tibet, and apart from the personnel sent there by the Central People's Government shall absorb as many local Tibetan personnel as possible to take part in the work. Local Tibetan personnel taking part in the military and administrative committee may include patriotic elements from the local government of Tibet, various districts and leading monasteries; the name-list shall be drawn up after consultation between the representatives designated by the Central People's Government and the various quarters concerned, and shall be submitted to the Central People's Government for appointment.

16. Funds needed by the military and administrative committee, the military area headquarters and the People's Liberation Army entering Tibet shall be provided by the Central People's Government. The local government of Tibet will assist the People's Liberation Army in the purchase and transport of food, fodder and other daily necessities.

17. This agreement shall come into force immediately after signatures and seals are affixed to it.

Signed and sealed by:

Delegates with full powers of the Central People's Government:

Chief Delegate:

Li Weihan

Delegates:

Zhang Jingwu

Zhang Guohua

Sun Zhiyuan

Delegates with full powers of the local government of Tibet:

Chief Delegate:

Galoon Ngapoi Ngwang Jigmei

Delegates:

Kemey Soinam Wangdui

Tubdain Dainda

Tubdain Lemoin

Sangpo Tainzin Toinzhub

Beijing, May 23, 1951

Appendix E

Five-Point Peace Plan

Address to the U.S. Congressional Human Rights Caucus
September 21, 1987

The world is increasingly interdependent, so that lasting peace - national, regional and global - can only be achieved if we think in terms of broader interest rather than parochial needs. At this time, it is crucial that all of us, the strong and the weak, contribute in our own way. I speak to you today as the leader of the Tibetan people and as a Buddhist monk devoted to the principles of a religion based on love and compassion. Above all, I am here as a human being who is destined to share this planet with you and all others as brothers and sisters. As the world grows smaller, we need each other more than in the past. This is true in all parts of the world, including the continent I come from.

At present in Asia, as elsewhere, tensions are high. There are open conflicts in the Middle East, Southeast Asia, and in my own country, Tibet. To a large extent, these problems are symptoms of the underlying tensions that exist among the area's great powers. In order to resolve regional conflicts, an approach is required that takes into account the interests of all relevant countries and peoples, large and small. Unless comprehensive solutions are formulated that take into account the aspirations of the people most directly concerned, piecemeal or merely expedient measures will only create new problems.

The Tibetan people are eager to contribute to regional and world peace, and I believe they are in a unique position to do so. Traditionally, Tibetans are a peace loving and non-violent people. Since Buddhism was introduced to Tibet over one thousand years ago, Tibetans have practiced non-violence with respect to all forms of life. This attitude has also been extended to our country's international relations. Tibet's highly strategic position in the heart of Asia, separating the continent's great powers - India, China and the USSR - has throughout history endowed it with an essential role in the maintenance of peace and stability. This is precisely why, in the past, Asia's empires went to great lengths to keep one another out of Tibet. Tibet's value as an independent buffer state was integral to the region's stability.

When the newly formed People's Republic of China invaded Tibet in 1949/50, it created a new source of conflict. This was highlighted when, following the Tibetan national uprising against the Chinese and my flight to India in 1959, tensions between China and India escalated into the border war in 1962. Today large numbers of troops are again massed on both sides of the Himalayan border and tension is once more dangerously high.

The real issue, of course, is not the Indo-Tibetan border demarcation. It is China's illegal occupation of Tibet, which has given it direct access to the Indian sub-continent. The Chinese authorities have attempted to confuse the issue by claiming that Tibet has always been a part of China. This is untrue. Tibet was a fully independent state when the People's Liberation Army invaded the country in 1949/50.

Since Tibetan emperors unified Tibet, over a thousand years ago, our country was able to maintain its independence until the middle of this century. At times Tibet extended its influence over neighbouring countries and peoples and, in other periods, came itself under the influence of powerful foreign rulers - the Mongol Khans, the Gorkhas of Nepal, the Manchu Emperors and the British in India.

It is, of course, not uncommon for states to be subjected to foreign influence or interference. Although so-called satellite relationships are perhaps the clearest examples of this, most major powers exert influence over less powerful allies or neighbours. As the most authoritative legal studies have shown, in Tibet's case, the country's occasional subjection to foreign influence never entailed a loss of independence. And there can be no doubt that when Peking's communist armies entered Tibet, Tibet was in all respects an independent state.

China's aggression, condemned by virtually all nations of the free world, was a flagrant violation of international law. As China's military occupation of Tibet continues, the world should remember that though Tibetans have lost their freedom, under international law Tibet today is still an independent state under illegal occupation. It is not my purpose to enter into a political/legal discussion here concerning Tibet's status. I just wish to emphasise the obvious and undisputed fact that we Tibetans are a distinct people with our own culture, language, religion and history. But for China's occupation, Tibet would still, today, fulfil its natural role as a buffer state maintaining and promoting peace in Asia.

It is my sincere desire, as well as that of the Tibetan people, to restore to Tibet her invaluable role, by converting the entire country - comprising the three provinces of U-Tsang, Kham and Amdo - once more into a place of stability, peace and harmony. In the best of Buddhist tradition, Tibet would extend its services and hospitality to all who further the cause of world peace and the well-being of mankind and the natural environment we share.

Despite the holocaust inflicted upon our people in the past decades of occupation, I have always strived to find a solution through direct and honest discussions with the Chinese. In 1982, following the change of leadership in China and the establishment of direct contacts with the government in Peking, I sent my representatives to Peking to open talks concerning the future of my country and people.

We entered the dialogue with the sincere and positive attitude and with the willingness to take into account the legitimate needs of the People's Republic of China. I hoped that this attitude would be reciprocated and that a solution could eventually be found which would satisfy and safeguard the aspirations and interests of both parties. Unfortunately, China has consistently responded to our efforts in a defensive manner, as though our detailing of Tibet's very real difficulties was criticism for its own sake.

To our even greater dismay, the Chinese government misused the opportunity for a genuine dialogue. Instead of addressing the real issues facing the six million Tibetan people, China has attempted to reduce the question of Tibet to a discussion of my own personal status.

It is against this background and in response to the tremendous support and encouragement I have been given by you and other persons I have met during this trip, that I wish today to clarify the principal issues and to propose, in a spirit of openness and conciliation, a first step towards a lasting solution. I hope this may contribute to a future of friendship and cooperation with all of our neighbours, including the Chinese people.

This peace plan contains five basic components:

1. Transformation of the whole of Tibet into a zone of peace;

2. Abandonment of China's population transfer policy which threatens the very existence of the Tibetans as a people;

3. Respect for the Tibetan people's fundamental human rights and democratic freedoms;

4. Restoration and protection of Tibet's natural environment and the abandonment of China's use of Tibet for the production of nuclear weapons and dumping of nuclear waste;

5. Commencement of earnest negotiations on the future status of Tibet and of relations between the Tibetan and Chinese peoples.

Let me explain these five components.

1. I propose that the whole of Tibet, including the eastern provinces of Kham and Amdo, be transformed into a zone of "Ahimsa", a Hindi term used to mean a state of peace and non-violence.

The establishment of such a peace zone would be in keeping with Tibet's historical role as a peaceful and neutral Buddhist nation and buffer state separating the continent's great powers. It would also be in keeping with Nepal's proposal to proclaim Nepal a peace zone and with China's declared support for such a proclamation. The peace zone proposed by Nepal would have a much greater impact if it were to include Tibet and neighbouring areas.

The establishment of a peace zone in Tibet would require withdrawal of Chinese troops and military installations from the country, which would enable India also to withdraw troops and military installations from the Himalayan regions bordering Tibet. This would be achieved under an international agreement which would satisfy China's legitimate security needs and build trust among the Tibetan, Indian, Chinese and other peoples of the region. This is in everyone's best interest, particularly that of China and India, as it would enhance their security, while reducing the economic burden of maintaining high troop concentrations on the disputed Himalayan border.

Historically, relations between China and India were never strained. It was only when Chinese armies marched into Tibet, creating for the first time a common border, that tensions arose between these two powers, ultimately leading to the 1962 war. Since then numerous incidents have continued to occur. A restoration of good relations between the world's two most populous countries would be greatly facilitated if they were separated - as they were throughout history - by a large and friendly buffer region.

To improve relations between the Tibetan people and the Chinese, the first requirement is the creation of trust. After the holocaust of the last decades in which over one million Tibetans - one sixth of the population - lost their lives and at least as many lingered in prison camps because of their religious beliefs and love of freedom, only a withdrawal of Chinese troops could start a genuine process of reconciliation. The vast occupation force in Tibet is a daily reminder to the Tibetans of the oppression and suffering they have all experienced. A troop withdrawal would be an essential signal that in future a meaningful relationship might be established with the Chinese, based on friendship and trust.

2. The population transfer of Chinese into Tibet, which the government in Peking pursues in order to force a "final solution" to the Tibetan problem by reducing the Tibetan population to an insignificant and disenfranchised minority in Tibet itself, must be stopped.

The massive transfer of Chinese civilians into Tibet in violation of the Fourth Geneva Convention (1949), threatens the very existence of the Tibetans as a distinct people. In the eastern parts of our country, the Chinese now greatly outnumber Tibetans. In the Amdo province, for example, where I was born, there are, according to the Chinese statistics, 2.5 million Chinese and only 750,000 Tibetans. Even in the so-called Tibet Autonomous Region (i.e., central and western Tibet), Chinese government sources now confirm that Chinese outnumber Tibetans.

The Chinese population transfer policy is not new. It has been systematically applied to other areas before. Earlier in this century, the Manchus were a distinct race with their own culture and traditions. Today only two to three million Manchurians are left in Manchuria, where 75 million Chinese have settled. In Eastern Turkestan, which the Chinese now call Sinkiang, the Chinese population has grown from 200,000 in 1949 to 7 million, more than half of the total population of 13 million. In the wake of the Chinese colonization of Inner Mongolia, Chinese number 8.5 million, Mongols 2.5 million.

Today, in the whole of Tibet 7.5 million Chinese settlers have already been sent, outnumbering the Tibetan population of 6 million. In central and western Tibet, now referred to by the Chinese as the "Tibet Autonomous Region", Chinese sources admit the 1.9 million Tibetans already constitute a minority of the region's population. These numbers do not take the estimated 300,000-500,000 troops in Tibet into account - 250,000 of them in so-called Tibet Autonomous Region.

For the Tibetans to survive as a people, it is imperative that the population transfer is stopped and Chinese settlers return to China. Otherwise, Tibetans will soon be no more than a tourist attraction and relic of a noble past.

3. Fundamental human rights and democratic freedoms must be respected in Tibet. The Tibetan people must once again be free to develop culturally, intellectually, economically and spiritually and to exercise basic democratic freedoms.

Human rights violations in Tibet are among the most serious in the world. Discrimination is practiced in Tibet under a policy of "apartheid" which the Chinese call "segregation and assimilation". Tibetans are, at best, second class citizens in their own country. Deprived of all basic democratic rights and freedoms, they exist under a colonial administration in which all real power is wielded by Chinese officials of the Communist Party and the army.

Although the Chinese government allows Tibetans to rebuild some Buddhist monasteries and to worship in them, it still forbids serious study and teaching of religion. Only a small number of people, approved by the Communist Party, are permitted to join the monasteries.

While Tibetans in exile exercise their democratic rights under a constitution promulgated by me in 1963, thousands of our countrymen suffer in prisons and labour camps in Tibet for their religious or political convictions.

4. Serious efforts must be made to restore the natural environment in Tibet. Tibet should not be used for the production of nuclear weapons and the dumping of nuclear waste.

Tibetans have a great respect for all forms of life. This inherent feeling is enhanced by the Buddhist faith, which prohibits the harming of all sentient beings, whether human or animal. Prior to the Chinese invasion, Tibet was an unspoiled wilderness sanctuary in a unique natural environment. Sadly, in the past decades the wildlife and the forests of Tibet have been almost totally destroyed by the Chinese. The effects on Tibet's delicate environment have been devastating. What little is left in Tibet must be protected and efforts must be made to restore the environment to its balanced state.

China uses Tibet for the production of nuclear weapons and may also have started   dumping nuclear waste in Tibet. Not only does China plan to dispose of its own nuclear waste but also that of other countries, who have already agreed to pay Peking to dispose of their toxic materials.

The dangers this presents are obvious. Not only living generations, but future generations are threatened by China's lack of concern for Tibet's unique and delicate environment.

5. Negotiations on the future status of Tibet and the relationship between the Tibetan and Chinese peoples should be started in earnest. We wish to approach this subject in a reasonable and realistic way, in a spirit of frankness and conciliation and with a view to finding a solution

that is in the long term interest of all: the Tibetans, the Chinese, and all other peoples concerned. Tibetans and Chinese are distinct peoples, each with their own country, history, culture, language, and way of life. Differences among peoples must be recognized and respected. They need not, however, form obstacles to genuine cooperation where this is in the mutual benefit of both peoples. It is my sincere belief that if the concerned parties were to meet and discuss their future with an open mind and a sincere desire to find a satisfactory and just solution, a breakthrough could be achieved. We must all exert ourselves to be reasonable and wise, and to meet in a spirit of frankness and understanding.

Let me end on the personal note. I wish to thank you for the concern and support which you and so many of your colleagues and fellow citizens have expressed for the plight of oppressed people everywhere. The fact that you have publicly shown your sympathy for us Tibetans, has already had a positive impact on the lives of our people inside Tibet. I ask for your continued support in this critical time in our country's history.

Thank you.

Appendix F

Strasbourg Proposal 1988

Address to the Members of the European Parliament
Strasbourg, France
June 15, 1988

We are living today in a very interdependent world. One nation's problem can no longer be solved by itself. Without a sense of universal responsibility our very survival is in danger. I have, therefore, always believed in the need for better understanding, closer co-operation, and greater respect among the various nations of the world. The European Parliament is an inspiring example. Out of the chaos of war, those who were once enemies have, in a single generation, learned to co-exist and to co-operate. I am, therefore, particularly pleased and honoured to address this gathering at the European Parliament.

As you know, my own country - Tibet - is undergoing a very difficult period. The Tibetans -particularly those who live under Chinese occupation - yearn for freedom and justice and a self-determined future, so that they are able to fully preserve their unique identity and live in peace with their neighbours. For over a thousand years, we Tibetans have adhered to spiritual and environmental values in order to maintain the delicate balance of life across the high plateau on which we live, inspired by Buddha's message of non-violence and compassion and protected by our mountains, we sought to respect every form of life and to abandon war as an instrument of national policy.

Our history, dating back more than two thousand years, has been one of independence. At no time, since the founding of our nation in 127 B.C., have we Tibetans conceded our sovereignty to a foreign power. As with all nations, Tibet experienced periods in which our neighbours - Mongol, Manchu, Chinese, British and the Gorkhas of Nepal - sought to establish influence over us. These eras have been brief and the Tibetan people have never accepted them as constituting a loss of national sovereignty. In fact, there have been occasions when Tibetans rulers conquered vast areas of China and other neighbouring states. This, however, does not mean that we Tibetans can lay claim to these territories.

In 1949 the People's Republic of China forcibly invaded Tibet. Since that time, Tibet has endured the darkest period in its history. More than a million of our people have died as a result of the occupation. Thousands of monasteries were reduced to ruins. A generation has grown up deprived of education, economic opportunities and a sense of its on national character. Though the current Chinese leadership has implemented certain reforms it is also promoting a massive population transfer onto the Tibetan plateau. This policy has already reduced the six million Tibetans to a minority. Speaking for all Tibetans, I must sadly inform you, our tragedy continues.

I have always urged my people not to resort to violence in their efforts to redress their sufferings. Yet I believe all people have a moral right to fully protest injustice. Unfortunately, the demonstrations in Tibet have been violently suppressed by the Chinese police and military. I will continue to counsel for non-violence, but unless China forsakes the brutal methods it employs, the Tibetans cannot be responsible for a further deterioration in the situation.

Every Tibetan hopes and prays for the full restoration of our nation's independence. Thousands of our people have sacrificed their lives and our whole nation has suffered in this struggle. Even in recent months, Tibetans have bravely sacrificed their lives to achieve this precious goal. On the other hand, the Chinese totally fail to recognize the Tibetan people's aspirations and continue to pursue a policy of brutal suppression.

I have thought for a long time on how to achieve a realistic solution to my nation's plight. My cabinet and I solicited the opinions of many friends and concerned persons. As a result, on September 21, 1987, at the Congressional Human Rights Caucus in Washington, D.C., I announced a Five Point Peace Plan for Tibet. In it I called for a conversion of Tibet into a zone of peace, a sanctuary in which humanity and nature can live together in harmony. I also called for respect of human rights, democratic ideals, environmental protection, and a halt to the Chinese population transfer into Tibet.

The fifth point of the peace plan called for earnest negotiations between the Tibetans and the Chinese. We, have therefore, taken the initiative to formulate some thoughts which, we hope, may serve as a basis for resolving the issue of Tibet. I would like to take this opportunity to inform the distinguished gathering here on the main points of our thinking.

The whole of Tibet known as Cholka-Sum (U-Tsang, Kham and Amdo) should become a self-governing democratic political entity founded on law by agreement of the people for the common good and the protection of themselves and their environment, in association with the People's Republic of China.

The Government of the People's Republic of China could remain responsible for Tibet's foreign policy. The Government of Tibet should, however, develop and maintain relations, through its own foreign affairs bureau, in the field of commerce, education, culture, religion, tourism, science, sports and other non-political activities. Tibet should join international organizations concerned with such activities.

The Government of Tibet should be founded on a constitution or basic law. The basic law should provide for a democratic system of government entrusted with the task of ensuring economic equality, social justice, and protection of the environment. This means that the Government of Tibet will have the rights to decide on all affairs relating to Tibet and the Tibetans.

As individual freedom is the real source and potential of any society's development, the Government of Tibet would seek to ensure this freedom by full adherence to the Universal Declaration of Human Rights, including the rights to speech, assembly and religion. Because religion constitutes the source of Tibet's national identity and spiritual values lie at the very heart of Tibet's rich culture, it would be the special duty of the Government of Tibet to safeguard and develop its practice.

The Government should be comprised of a popularly elected Chief Executive, a bi-cameral legislative branch, and an independent judicial system. Its seat should be in Lhasa.

The social and economic system of Tibet should be determined in accordance with the wishes of the Tibetan people, bearing in mind especially the need to raise the standard of living of the entire population.

The Government of Tibet would pass strict laws to protect wildlife and plantlife. The exploitation of natural resources would be carefully regulated. The manufacture, testing, stockpiling of nuclear weapons and other armaments must be prohibited, as well as use of nuclear power and other technologies which produce hazardous waste. It would be the Government of Tibet's goal to transform Tibet into our planet's largest natural preserve.

A regional peace conference should be called to ensure that Tibet becomes a genuine sanctuary of peace through demilitarization. Until such a peace conference can be convened and demilitarization and neutralization achieved, China could have the right to maintain a restricted number of military installations in Tibet. These must be solely for defence purposes.

In order to create an atmosphere of trust conductive to fruitful negotiations, the Chinese Government should cease its human rights violations in Tibet and abandon its policy of transferring Chinese to Tibet.

These are thoughts we have in mind. I am aware that many Tibetans will be disappointed by the moderate stand they represent. Undoubtedly, there will be much discussion in the coming months within our own community, both in Tibet and in exile. This, however, is an essential and invaluable part of any process of change. I believe these thoughts represent the most realistic means by which to re-establish Tibet's separate identity and restore the fundamental rights of Tibetan people while accommodating China's own interest. I would like to emphasize, however, that whatever the outcome of the negotiations with the Chinese may be, the Tibetan people themselves must be the ultimate deciding authority. Therefore, any proposal will contain a comprehensive procedural plan to ascertain the wishes of the Tibetan people in a nationwide referendum.

I would like to take this opportunity to state that I do not wish to take active part in the Government of Tibet. Nevertheless, I will continue to work as much as I can for the well-being and happiness of the Tibetan people as long as it is necessary.

We are ready to present a proposal to the Government of the People's Republic of China based on the thoughts I have presented. A negotiating team representing the Tibetan Government has been selected. We are prepared to meet with the Chinese to discuss details of such a proposal aimed at achieving an equitable solution.

We are encouraged by the keen interest being shown in our situation by a growing number of governments and political leaders, including former President Jimmy Carter of the United States. We are encouraged by the recent changes in China which have brought about a new group of leadership, more pragmatic and liberal.

We urge the Chinese Government and leadership to give serious and substantive consideration to the ideas I have described. Only dialogue and a willingness to look with honesty and clarity at the reality of Tibet can lead to a viable solution. We wish to conduct discussion with the Chinese Government bearing in mind the larger interests of humanity. Our proposal will therefore be made in a spirit of conciliation and we hope that the Chinese will respond accordingly.

My country's unique history and profound spiritual heritage render it ideally suited for fulfilling the role of a sanctuary of peace at the heart of Asia. Its historic status as a neutral buffer state, contributing to the stability of the entire continent, can be restored. Peace and security for Asia as well as for the world at large can be enhanced. In the future, Tibet need no longer be an occupied land, oppressed by force, unproductive and scarred by suffering. It can become a free haven where humanity and nature live in harmonious balance; a creative model for the resolution of tensions afflicting many areas throughout the world.

The Chinese leadership need to realize that colonial rule over occupied territories is today anachronistic. A large genuine union of association can only come about voluntarily, when there is satisfactory benefit to all the parties concerned. The European Community is a clear example of this. On the other hand, even one country or community can break into two or more entities where there is lack of trust or benefit, and when force is used as the principal means of rule.

I would like to end by making a special appeal to the honourable members of the European Parliament and through them to their respective constituencies to extend their support to our efforts. A resolution of the Tibetan problem within the framework that we proposed will not only be for the mutual benefit of the Tibetans and Chinese people but will contribute to regional and global peace and stability. I thank you for providing the opportunity to share my thoughts with you.

Thank you.

BIBLIOGRAPHY

Aiming, Zhou 2004: *Tibetan Education.* Beijing: China Intercontinental Press.

Amnesty International 1987: *Amnesty International : Le Rapport 1987.* Paris: La Découverte.

— 1988: *Amnesty International Rapport 1988.* Paris: Editions Francophones d'Amnesty International.

— 1989: *Amnesty International Rapport.* Paris: Editions francophones d'Amnesty International.

— 1997: *Amnesty International Report 1997.* www.ecoi.net/en/document/2023933.html [12.07.2021].

— 2009: *Amnesty International Report. The state of the world's human rights.* London: Amnesty International Publications.

— 2021: *Amnesty International Report 2020/21; The state of the world's human rights; China 2020.* www.ecoi.net/en/document/2048658.html [27.06.2021].

Angle, Stephen C. 2002: *Human Rights and the Chinese Thought: A Cross-Cultural Inquiry.* Cambridge: Cambridge University Press.

Appleby, R. Scott 2000: *The Ambivalence of the Sacred : Religion, Violence, and Reconciliation.* Rowman & Littlefield Publishers, INC.: Maryland.

Avedon, John F. 1985: *In Exile from the Land of Snows.* London: Wisdom Publications.

Barnett, Robert 1999: *Essai.* In: Lehman, Steve: *Les Tibétains en lutte pour leur survie.* Paris: Editions Hoëbeke: 178-196.

— 2008: *What were the conditions regarding human rights in Tibet before democratic reform?* In: Blondeau, Anne-Marie; Buffetrille, Katia: *Authenticating Tibet: Answers to China's 100 questions.* Berkeley: University of California Press: 81-84.

— 2008: *Some foreign newspapers have claimed that the Chinese killed more than 1 million Tibetans. Is this true?* In: Blondeau, Anne-Marie; Buffetrille, Katia: *Authenticating Tibet: Answers to China's 100 questions.* Berkeley: University of California Press: 88-90.

Basu, Sudeep 2012: *Interrogating Tibetan Exilic Culture: Issues and Concerns.* Sociological Bulletin 61, no. 2 (2012): 232-254. www.jstor.org/stable/23620966 [20/04/2017].

Baumann, Jonas; Finnbogason, Daniel; Svensson, Isak 2018: *Rethinking Mediation: Resolving Religious Conflicts. CSS Policy Perspectives, 6(1).* Center for Security Studies (CSS), ETH Zurich.

Baumgartner, Elisabeth; Ott, Lisa 2017: *Determining the Fate of Missing Persons. The importance of Archives for "Dealing with the Past" Mechanisms.* In: International Review of the Red Cross, 99 (2): 663-688.

Bitter, Jean-Nicolas 2011: *Transforming Conflicts with Religious Dimensions.* In: *Religion in Conflict Transformation, Politorbis No. 52.* Swiss FDFA: 27-32.

Bonnin, Michel; Hall, Jonathan 2007: *The Threatened History and Collective Memory of the Cultural Revolution's Lost Generation.* http://jstor.org/stable/24052854 [06.07.2019].

Boss, Pauline 2006: *Loss, Trauma, and Resilience: Therapeutic Work With Ambiguous Loss.* New York: W. W. Norton and Compagny.

Bruno, Ellen 1993: *Satya: a prayer for the enemy* [Documentary]. New Jersey: Film Library.

— 2005; *Sky Burial* [Documentary]. New Jersey: Film Library.

Buffetrille, Katia; RAMBLE, Charles 1998: *Tibétains : 1959-1999 : 40 Ans de Colonisation.* Paris: Autrement.

— 2008: *Do the Tibetan and Han People enjoy equal payment for same work?.* In: Blondeau, Anne-Marie; Buffetrille, Katia: *Authenticating Tibet: Answers to China's 100 questions.* Berkeley: University of California Press: 301-302.

Cencetti, Elisa 2011: *Tibetan Plateau Grassland Protection: Tibetan Herders' Ecological Conception Versus State Policies.* Himalaya 30(1). https://digitalcommons.macalester.edu/himalaya/vol30/iss1/12 [26.05.2020].

CDA 2015: *Conflict Analysis Framework: Field Guidelines and Procedures.* The Hague: GPPAC.

Changching, Cao 2015: *Brainwashing the Chinese.* In: Changching, Cao; Seymour, James D: *Tibet through Dissident Chinese Eyes. Essays on Self-Determination.* London: Routledge: 25-30.

Chaumont, Jean-Michel 1997: *La concurrence des victimes : Génocides, identité, reconnaissance.* Paris: Editions La Découvertes.

Chayet, Anne 2008: *Are there any historical documents which provide evidence that Tibet is part of China?* In: Blondeau, Anne-Marie; Buffetrille, Katia: *Authenticating Tibet: Answers to China's 100 questions.* Berkeley: University of California Press: 37-38.

China Daily 2007: *Rule on living Buddhas aids religious freedom.* www.chinadaily.com.cn/china/2007-12/27/content_6351750.htm [21/12/2020].

Christian Solidarity Worldwide 30 April 2021: *New regulations described as 'one more weapon' to restrict religious communities.* www.ecoi.net/en/document/2050505.html [24 May 2021].

Congressional-Executive Commission on China, 10 October 2018, *Annual Report 2018.* www.ecoi.net/en/document/1445882.html [22.04.2021].

Congressional-Executive Commission on China 10 October 2010: *Annual Report 2010.* www.cecc.gov/sites/chinacommission.house.gov/files/2010%20CECC%20Annual%20Report.PDF [26.08.2021].

Congressional-Executive Commission on China 30 September 2020: *"The Human Rights Situation in Tibet and the International Response" Hearing by the Congressional Executive Commission on China, September 30, 2020; Testimony by Matteo Mecacci; President, International Campaign for Tibet.* www.ecoi.net/en/document/2040131.html [06.04.2021].

Croix-Rouge suisse 1967: *Rapport Annuel de la Croix-Rouge suisse.* Berne: Croix-Rouge suisse.

— 1971: *Rapport Annuel de la Croix-Rouge suisse.* Berne: Croix-Rouge suisse.

—   1985: *Rapport Annuel de la Croix-Rouge suisse.* Berne: Croix-Rouge suisse.

Dalai Lama, His Holiness the, 2016: My Land and My People. New Delhi: Timeless Books.

Dhondup Wangchen; Golok Jigme 2008: *Leave fear behind* [Documentary].

Department of Information and International Relation 2016: *Middle Way Policy and All Recent Related Documents.* Dharamshala: DIIR, Central Tibetan Administration.

—   2018: *Human Rights Violations: The Case of Tibet.* Dharamshala: DIIR, Central Tibetan Administration (1).

—   2018: *Tibet was never a part of China but The Middle Way Approach Remains a Viable Solution.* Dharamshala: DIIR, Central Tibetan Administration (2).

Epstein, Israel 1983: *Tibet Transformed.* Beijing: New World Press.

Federal Department of Foreign Affairs, Human Security Division 2018: *Dealing with the Past.* Bern. www.eda.admin.ch/eda/en/home/foreign-policy/human-rights/peace/dealing-with-past.html [27.07.2020].

Fox, Jonathan 2002: *Ethnoreligious Conflict in the Late Twentieth Century.* Lexington Books: Lanham.

Freedom House 2021: *Freedom in the World 2021 – Tibet.* www.ecoi.net/en/document/2052873.html [20.06.2021].

Human Rights House 26 October 2009: *China executes four Tibetans over spring 2008 protest.* https://humanrightshouse.org/articles/china-executes-four-tibetans-over-spring-2008-protest/ [25.06.2021].

Gandolfi, Stefania; Sow, Abdoulaye; Bieger-Merkli, Caroline; Meyer-Bisch, Patrice 2008: *Droits culturels et traitement des violences: Actes du colloque international Université de Nouakchott, 9-11 novembre 2007*. Paris: L'Harmattan.

Global Times 2020: *US Tibet bill interference in China's internal affairs*. *www.globaltimes.cn/content/1177961.shtml* [29.04. 2020].

Gopin, Marc 2015: *Negotiating Secular and Religious Contributions*. In: Omer, Atalia; Appleby, R. Scott; Little, David: *The Oxford Handbook of Religion, Conflict, and Peacebuilding*. Oxford: Oxford University Press: 355-379.

Goetschel, Laurent 2009: *Conflict Transformation*. In: Chetail, Vincent (ed.): *Post-Conflict Peacebuilding. A Lexicon*. Oxford, Oxford University Press: 92-104.

Goldstein, Melvyn C. 1997: *The snow lion and the dragon: China, Tibet, and the Dalai Lama*. Berkeley: University of California Press.

Grunfeld, Tom A. 1987: *The Making of Modern Tibet*. London: Zed Books Ltd.

Hambourg, D. A. 2010: *Preventing Genocide: Practical Steps Toward Early Detection and Effective Action*. London: Paradigm Publishers.

Hayner, Priscilla 2006: *The Power of Memory and the Difficulty of Truth: Assessing Recent Experience*. In: Bleeker, Mô 2006: *Dealing with the Past and Transitional Justice: Creating Conditions for Peace, Human Rights and the Rule of Law*. Conference Paper 1/2006 Dealing with the Past – Series. Bern: Political Affairs Division IV, Federal Department of Foreign Affairs FDFA: 43-48.

Heath, John 2005: *Tibet and China in the Twenty-first Century: nonviolence versus state power*. London: Saqibooks.

Heller, Amy; Blondeau, Anne-Marie 2008: *How about the use of the Tibetan language?* In: Blondeau, Anne-Marie; Buffetrille, Katia: *Authenticating Tibet: Answers to China's 100 questions*. Berkeley: University of California Press: 234-236.

Human Rights Watch 2009: *"An Alleyway in Hell": China's Abusive "Black Jails"*. www.hrw.org/report/2009/11/12/alleyway-hell/chinas-abusive-black-jails [30.07.2020].

—   2010: *"I Saw It with My Own Eyes": Abuses by Chinese Security Forces in Tibet, 2008-2010*. www.hrw.org/report/2010/07/21/i-saw-it-my-own-eyes/abuses-chinese-security-forces-tibet-2008-2010 [03.11.2020].

—   2013: *"They Say We Should Be Grateful". Mass Rehousing and Relocation Programs in Tibetan Areas of China*. www.hrw.org/report/2013/06/27/they-say-we-should-be-grateful/mass-rehousing-and-relocation-programs-tibetan [29.07.2020].

—   2014: *China: 1,000 Evictions from Tibetan Buddhist Centers*. https://bit.ly/38fOYjW [06.04.2021].

—   2018: *"Eradicating Ideological Viruses": China's Campaign of Repression Against Xinjiang's Muslims*. www.refworld.org/cgi-bin/texis/vtx/rwmain?page=search&docid=5badfce54&skip=0&query=Xinjiang&coi=CHN [05.04.2021].

—   2016: *Relentless: Detention and Prosecution of Tibetans under China's "Stability Maintenance" Campaign*. www.ecoi.net/en/document/1346260.html [14.10.2019].

— 2020: *Silenced in China: The Archivists.* www.hrw.org/news/2020/07/22/silenced-china-archivists [29.07.2020].

Immigration and Refugee Board of Canada 6 October 2020: *China, India, Nepal: Situation and treatment of Tibetans in China; treatment of returnees to China, including returnees from India and Nepal (2017–October 2020) [ZZZ200323.E].* www.ecoi.net/en/document/2039983.html [06.04.2021].

International Campaign for Tibet 13 January 2021: *Self-Immolation Fact Sheet.* https://savetibet.org/tibetan-self-immolations/ [07.04.2021].

International Commission oF Jurists 1959: *The Question of Tibet and the Rule of Law.* www.icj.org/wp-content/uploads/1959/01/Tibet-rule-of-law-report-1959-eng.pdf [16/03/2020].

International Commission of Jurists 1960: *Tibet and the Chinese People's Republic.* www.icj.org/el-tibet-y-la-republica-popular-de-china-el/ [16.03.2020].

Juergensmeyer, Mark 2011: *Rethinking the Secular and Religious Aspects of Violence,* In: Calhoun, Craig; Juergensmeyer, Mark; Van Antwerpen, Jonathan: *Rethinking Secularism.* Oxford University Press, New York, 185-203.

Jones, Ken 1989: *The social face of Buddhism: an approach to political and social activism.* London: Wisdom Publications.

Kessel, Jonah M. 2015: *Tashi Wangchuk: A Tibetan's Journey for Justice* [Documentary]. In: New York Times, 28 November 2015. www.nytimes.com/video/world/asia/100000004031427/a-tibetans-journey-for-justice.html [23.07.2020].

King, Sallie B. 2012: *Buddhism and Human Rights.* In: WITTE, John Jr.; GREEN, Christian M.: *Religion and human rights: an introduction.* New York: Oxford University Press: 103-118.

Koller, Frédéric 2015: *Ces suppliciés tibétains des JO de Pékin.* In : Le Temps, 2 October 2015, www.letemps.ch/monde/ supplicies-tibetains-jo-pekin [03.03.2020].

Kopf, David 1999: *Tibet, Genocide by China In.* In: Charny, Israel W.: *Encyclopedia of Genocide Volume I & II*, Santa Barbara: ABC-CLIO: 543.

Lederach, John Paul 2003: *The little book of conflict transformation: Clear articulation of the guiding principles by pioneer in the field.* Intercourse: Good Books. https://professorbellreadings. files.wordpress.com/2017/10/the-little-books-of-justice-peacebuilding-john-lederach-the-little-book-of-conflict-transformation-good-books-2014-1.pdf [31.08.2021].

Legal Inquiry Committee on Tibet 1960: *Tibet and the Chinese People's Republic: A report to the International Commission of Jurists.* Geneva: International Commission of Jurists.

Lemkin, Raphael 1944: *Axis rule in occupied Europe: Laws of Occupation, Analysis of Government, Proposals for Redress.* Washington: Carnegie Endowment for International Peace.

Liming, Song 2015: *Reflections on the Seventeen-point Agreement of 1951.* In: Changching, Cao; Seymour, James D.: *Tibet through Dissident Chinese Eyes. Essays on Self-Determination.* London: Routledge: 55-70.

Lizhl, Fang 2015: *Tibetan, Chinese, and Human Rights.* In: Changching, Cao; Seymour, James D.: *Tibet through Dissident Chinese Eyes. Essays on Self-Determination.* London: Routledge: 37-40.

Macek, Ivana 2014: *Engaging violence: trauma, self-reflection and knowledge*. In: Macek, Ivana: *Engaging violence: trauma, memory and representation*. London: Routledge: 1-24.

Mann, Michael 2005: *The Dark Side of Democracy: explaining ethnic cleansing*. Cambridge: Cambridge University Press.

Margolin, Jean-Louis 2008: *Mao's China: The Worst Non-Genocidal Regime?* In: Stone, Dan: *The Historiography of Genocide*. Basingstoke: Palgrave Macmillan: 438-467.

Meyer-Bisch, Patrice; Bidault, Mylène 2010: *Déclarer les droits culturels: Commentaires de la Déclaration de Fribourg*. Genève: Schulthess. Bruxelles: Bruylant.

Morel, Fanny Iona 2016: *The denial of cultural rights as a weapon of domination*. Observatory of diversity and cultural rights: Fribourg. www.ohchr.org/FR/Issues/CulturalRights/Pages/Intentionaldestructionofculturalheritage.aspx [03.11.2020].

Morin, Edgar; Julien, Claude; Vasak, Karel; Jacot-Guillarmod, Olivier; Burgel, Guy; Faye, Jean-Pierre; Widmer, Jean; Villet, Maurice; Pinto de Oliveira, Carlos-Josaphat; Meyer-Bisch, Patrice 1987: *Forces et faiblesses des totalitarismes*. Éditions Universitaires: Fribourg.

National Geographic 2013: *Sky Burials: Tradition Becomes Controversial Tourist Attraction* [Documentary]. https://video.nationalgeographic.com/video/short-film-showcase/00000152-3c2a-d480-a756-7fee08570000 [17.12.2019].

Ngo, Tam; Smyer Yu, Dan; Van der Veer, Peter 2015: *Religion and Peace in Asia*. In: Omer, Atalia; Appleby, R. Scott; Little, David: *The Oxford Handbook of Religion, Conflict, and Peacebuilding*. Oxford: Oxford University Press: 407-429.

Nic Craith, Mairead 2010: *Linguistic heritage and language rights in Europe: Theoretical consideration and practical implications*. In: Langfield, Michele; Logan, William; Nic Craith, Mairead: *Cultural diversity, heritage and human rights: intersections in theory and practice*. London: Routledge: 45-62.

Omer, Atalia 2015: *Religion, Nationalism, and Solidarity Activism*. In: OMER, Atalia; Appleby, R. Scott; Little, David: *The Oxford Handbook of Religion, Conflict, and Peacebuilding*. Oxford: Oxford University Press: 611-655.

Postiglione, Gerad A.; Jiao, Ben 2009: *Tibet's relocated schooling: Popularization Reconsidered. Asian Survey,* 49 (5): 895-914. https://doi.org/10.1525/as.2009.49.5.895 [26.05.2020].

Qingying, Chen 2004: *L'Histoire du Tibet*. Beijing: China Intercontinental Press.

Roberts, John B.; Roberts, Elizabeth A. 2009: *Freeing Tibet: 50 years of struggle, resilience, and hope*. New York: Amacom.

Roemer, Stephanie 2010: *The Tibetan Government-in-Exile: Politics at large*. London: Routledge advances in South Asian Studies.

Rosenberg, Marshall B. 2015: *Nonviolent Communication: A Language of Life*. Encinitas: PuddleDancer Press.

Ruowang, Wang 2015: *The Status of Tibet: Recalling a Visit to Lhasa*. In: Changching, Cao; Seymour, James D.: *Tibet through Dissident Chinese Eyes. Essays on Self-Determination*. London: Routledge: 71-74.

Ruwitch, John 2008: *China vows to compensate victims in Lhasa violence.* Reuters, 29 March 2008. www.reuters.com/article/idINIndia-32746520080329 [15.04.2021].

Schnapper, Dominique 2008: *Mémoire et identité au temps de la construction européenne.* In: Schnapper, Dominique; Von Bülow, Katarina; Möller, Horst; Garton Ash, Timothy 2008: *Identity and Memory.* Paris: Collection penser l'Europe: 71.

Sen, Amartya Kumar 2007: *Identity and Violence: The Illusion of Destiny.* London: Penguin.

Shakya, Tsering 1999: *The dragon in the land of snows: a history of modern Tibet since 1947.* London: Pimlico.

Short, Damien 2016: *Redefining Genocide: Settler Colonialism, Social Death and Ecocide.* London: Zed Books.

Smith, Warren W. Jr. 2008: *China's Tibet? Autonomy or Assimilation.* Lanham: Rowman & Littlefield Publishers, Inc.

Sodnamkyid; Sulek, Emilia Roza 2017: *'Everything costs money': Livelihood and economics in the 'New resettled village' of Sogrima, Golok (Qinghai Province).* Nomadic Peoples, 21 (1): 136-151.

Sperling, Elliot 2009: *Tibet and China: The Interpretation of History Since 1950.* http://journals.openedition.org/chinaperspectives/4839 [16/10/2019].

Statista; National Bureau of Statistics of China 2019: *Illiteracy rate in China in 2018, by region.* www.statista.com/statistics/278568/illiteracy-rate-in-china-by-region/ [04.08.2020].

Strong, Anna Louise 1976: *When Serfs Stood Up in Tibet.* San Francisco: Red Sun Publishers.

Sulek, Emilia Roza 2016: *New urban proletariat.* The Newsletter, No. 75: 4-5.

Swiss Federal Archives, E1004.1#1000/9#800*, Beschlussprotokolle des Bundesrates November, 1973-1973. http://dodis.ch/37714 [31.07.2017].

Swiss Federal Archives, E2001E-01#1987/78#2323*, B. 15.21.(1) Uch, Besuch BR Graber in China, August 1974: Diverse Handakten, 1973-1975. http://dodis.ch/37704 [31.07.2017].

Swisspeace 2016: *A Conceptual Framework for Dealing with the Past.* Bern: Swisspeace.

Tibetan Centre for Human Rights and Democracy 16 June 2020: *2019 Annual Report on Human Rights Situation in Tibet.* www.ecoi.net/en/document/2032430.html [06.04.2021].

Tibet Information Network 1997: *A Poisoned Arrow: The Secret Report of the 10th Panchen Lama.* London: Tibet Information Network.

UN News 9 September 2014: *Peace means dignity, well-being for all, not just absence of war – UN officials.* https://news.un.org/en/story/2014/09/476992-peace-means-dignity-well-being-all-not-just-absence-war-un-officials [05.04.2021].

United Nations 2014: *Framework of Analysis for Atrocity Crimes: A Tool for Prevention.* New York: United Nations Office on Genocide Prevention and the Responsibility to Protect. www.un.org/en/genocideprevention/documents/about-us/Doc.3_Framework%20of%20Analysis%20for%20Atrocity%20Crimes_EN.pdf [28.08.2021].

Unrepresented Nations & Peoples Organization 23 May 2018: *Tibet Member Profile.* https://unpo.org/members/7879 [15.04.2021].

United States Department of State 30 January 1997: *U.S. Department of State Country Report on Human Rights Practices 1996 – China.* www.refworld.org/docid/3ae6aa79c.html [06.04.2021].

—   20 April 2018: *Country Report on Human Rights Practices 2017 - China (Tibet).* www.ecoi.net/en/document/1430193.html [06.04.2021].

—   21 June 2019: *2018 Report on International Religious Freedom: China-Tibet.* www.ecoi.net/en/document/2011121.html [06.04.2021].

—   30 March 2021: *2020 Country Report on Human Rights Practices: China (Tibet).* www.ecoi.net/en/document/2048116.html [06.04.2021].

—   May 2021: *2020 Report on International Religious Freedom: China.* www.ecoi.net/en/document/2051558.html [19.06.2021].

—   May 2021: *2020 Report on International Religious Freedom: China – Tibet.* www.state.gov/reports/2020-report-on-international-religious-freedom/china/tibet/ [03.07.2021].

United States Congress Senate 23 April 2008: *The Crisis in Tibet: Finding a Path to Peace.* www.govinfo.gov/app/details/CHRG-110shrg47764/context [15.04.2021].

United States Senate Committee on Foreign Relations 4 December 2018, *Testimony of Deputy Assistant Secretary Scott Busby.* www.foreign.senate.gov/imo/media/doc/120418_Busby_Testimony.pdf [05.04.2021].

Walsh, William C. 2014: *Know Your Rights: What is Freedom of Religion?* OSCE Institute on Religion and Public Policy: 1-12.

Walton, Matthew J.; Hayward, A. Susan 2014: *Contesting Buddhist Narratives. Democratization, Nationalism, and Communal Violence in Myanmar.* Policy Studies No. 71, Honolulu: East-West Center: 1-27.

Van Walt Van Praag, Michael; Boltjes, Mieck 2020: *Tibet Brief 20/20.* Denver: Outskirts Press.

Wimmer, Andreas 1996: *The resettlement of refugees: an analysis of the Swiss experience in the internatinal [sic] context.* Neuchâtel: Forum Suisse pour l'étude des migrations.

Xiangmei, Li; Ahamed, Selena 2018: *"Stability Maintenance" Campaign or "New Socialist Countryside" Campaign? China's Relocated Programs in Tibetan Plateau. https://aag.secure-abstracts.com/AAG%20Annual%20Meeting%202018/abstracts-gallery/252* [26/11/2019].

Xinhua News Agency 2020: *Tibet receives 40 million tourists in 2019.* www.globaltimes.cn/content/1176126.shtml [10.05.2020].

Yao, Wang 1996: *Hu Yaobang's visit to Tibet, May 22-31, 1980.* In Barnett, Robert; Akiner, Shirin: *Resistance and reform in Tibet.* Delhi: Motilal Banarsidass: 285-289.

Yuwel, Hu 2020: *Tibet government first in China to legislate ethnic unity guarantee.* www.globaltimes.cn/content/1176551.shtml [23/01/2020].

Zilin, Ding; Peikun, Jiang 2015: *Tibetans' Rights and Chinese Intellectuals' Responsibility.* In: Changching, Cao; Seymour,

James D.: *Tibet through Dissident Chinese Eyes. Essays on Self-Determination.* London: Routledge: 31-35.

Official Documents, Laws and Treaties

Central People's Government 1951: *The Agreement of the Central People's Government and the Local Government of Tibet on Measures for the Peaceful Liberation of Tibet.* www.china.org.cn/english/zhuanti/tibet%20facts/163877.htm [28.09.2019].

Constitution of the People's Republic of China, 4 December 1982. www.refworld.org/docid/4c31ea082.html [11.07.2021].

Dalai Lama, His Holiness, 1987: *Five Point Peace Plan.* www.dalailama.com/messages/tibet/five-point-peace-plan [03.11.2020].

Dalai Lama, His Holiness, 1988: *Strasbourg Proposal.* www.dalailama.com/messages/tibet/strasbourg-proposal-1988 [03.11.2020].

Tibetan Policy and Support Act of 2019 - H.R.4331 - 116th Congress 2020: *Tibetan Policy and Support Act of 2019.* www.congress.gov/bill/116th-congress/house-bill/4331/text [21/12/2020].

Observatory of Diversity and Cultural Rights, 2007: *Cultural Rights, Fribourg Declaration.* https://droitsculturels.org/observatoire/la-declaration-de-fribourg/ [13.06.2015].

State Administration for Religious Affairs 2007: *Measures on the Management of the Reincarnation of Living Buddhas in Tibetan Buddhism.* www.cecc.gov/resources/legal-provisions/measures-on-the-management-of-the-reincarnation-of-living-buddhas-in-0 [15.09.2020].

UNESCO 2001: *Universal Declaration on Cultural Diversity.* http://portal.unesco.org/fr/ev.php-URL_ID=13179&URL_DO=DO_TOPIC&URL_SECTION=201.html [03.11.2019].

— 2005: *Convention on the Protection and Promotion of the Diversity of Cultural Expressions.* http://portal.unesco.org/en/ev.php-URL_ID=31038&URL_DO=DO_TOPIC&URL_SECTION=201.html [03.11.2019].

United Nations, 1948: *Universal Declaration of Human Rights.* www.un.org/en/universal-declaration-human-rights/ [13.06.2015].

— 1948: *Convention on the Prevention and Punishment of the Crime of Genocide.* www.un.org/en/genocideprevention/genocide-convention.shtml [26.03.2016].

— 1966: *United Nations International Covenant on Economic, Social and Cultural Rights.* www.ohchr.org/en/professionalinterest/pages/cescr.aspx [13.06.2015].

— 2007: *United Nations Declaration on the Rights of Indigenous Peoples.* www.un.org/development/desa/indigenouspeoples/declaration-on-the-rights-of-indigenous-peoples.html [03.11.2020].

— General Assembly 2014: *Report of the Special Rapporteur in the field of cultural rights, Farida Shaheed Memorialization processes.* A/HRC/25/49. http://undocs.org/en/A/HRC/25/49 [05.06.2016].

— General Assembly 2014: *Summary of panel discussion on history teaching and memorialization processes. Report of the United Nations High Commissioner for Human Rights.*

A/HRC/28/36. http://undocs.org/en/A/HRC/28/36 [07.01. 2019].

— General Assembly 2018: *Free, prior and informed consent: a human rights-based approach.* A/HRC/39/62. https://undocs.org/en/A/HRC/39/62 [05.04.2021].

— General Assembly 2017: *Report of the Special Rapporteur on the promotion of truth, justice, reparation and guarantees of non-recurrence.* A/HRC/36/50. http://undocs.org/en/ A/HRC/36/50 [07.01.2019].

— General Assembly 2020: *Report of the Working Group on Enforced or Involuntary Disappearances.* A/HRC/45/13 [03.12.2020].

Globethics.net Publications

The list below is only a selection of our publications. To view the full collection, please visit our website.

All products are provided free of charge and can be downloaded in PDF form from the Globethics.net library and at www.globethics.net/publications. Bulk print copies can be ordered from publictions@globethics.net at special rates for those from the Global South.
Paid products not provided free of charge are indicated[*].
The Editor of the different Series of Globethics.net Publications is Prof. Dr Obiora Ike, Executive Director of Globethics.net in Geneva and Professor of Ethics at the Godfrey Okoye University Enugu/Nigeria.

Contact for manuscripts and suggestions: publications@globethics.net

Co-publications & Other

Kenneth R. Ross, *Mission Rediscovered: Transforming Disciples*, 2020, 138pp. ISBN 978-2-88931-369-3

Obiora Ike, Amélé Adamavi-Aho Ekué, Anja Andriamay, Lucy Howe López (Eds.), *Who Cares About Ethics?* 2020, 352pp. ISBN 978-2-88931-381-5

Obiora Ike, *Faith and Action Rooted in Christ Reflections on Spirituality, Justice, and Ethical Living*, 2021, 389pp, ISBN 978-2-88931-415-7

Global Series

Christoph Stückelberger / Jesse N.K. Mugambi (eds.), *Responsible Leadership. Global and Contextual Perspectives*, 2007, 376pp. ISBN: 978–2–8254–1516–0

Heidi Hadsell / Christoph Stückelberger (eds.), *Overcoming Fundamentalism. Ethical Responses from Five Continents*, 2009, 212pp.
ISBN: 978–2–940428–00–7

Ariane Hentsch Cisneros / Shanta Premawardhana (eds.), *Sharing Values. A Hermeneutics for Global Ethics*, 2010, 418pp.
ISBN: 978–2–940428–25–0.

Education Ethics Series

Divya Singh / Christoph Stückelberger (Eds.), *Ethics in Higher Education Values-driven Leaders for the Future*, 2017, 367pp. ISBN: 978–2–88931–165–1

Obiora Ike / Chidiebere Onyia (Eds.) *Ethics in Higher Education, Foundation for Sustainable Development*, 2018, 645pp. IBSN: 978-2-88931-217-7

Obiora Ike / Chidiebere Onyia (Eds.) *Ethics in Higher Education, Religions and Traditions in Nigeria* 2018, 198pp. IBSN: 978-2-88931-219-1

Obiora F. Ike, Justus Mbae, Chidiebere Onyia (Eds.), *Mainstreaming Ethics in Higher Education: Research Ethics in Administration, Finance, Education, Environment and Law Vol. 1*, 2019, 779pp. ISBN 978-2-88931-300-6

Ikechukwu J. Ani/Obiora F. Ike (Eds.), *Higher Education in Crisis Sustaining Quality Assurance and Innovation in Research through Applied Ethics*, 2019, 214pp. ISBN 978-2-88931-323-5

Deivit Montealegre / María Eugenia Barroso (Eds.), *Ethics in Higher Education, a Transversal Dimension: Challenges for Latin America. Ética en educación superior, una dimensión transversal: Desafíos para América Latina*, 2020, 148pp. ISBN 978-2-88931-359-4

Obiora Ike, Justus Mbae, Chidiebere Onyia, Herbert Makinda (Eds.), *Mainstreaming Ethics in Higher Education Vol. 2*, 2021, 420pp. ISBN: 978-2-88931-383-9

Christoph Stückelberger/ Joseph Galgalo/ Samuel Kobia (Eds.), *Leadership with Integrity. Higher Education from Vocation to Funding*, 2021, 288pp. ISBN 978-2-88931-389-1

Theses Series

Sabina Kavutha Mutisya, *The Experience of Being a Divorced or Separated Single Mother: A Phenomenological Study*, 2019, 168pp. ISBN: 978-2-88931-274-0

Florence Muia, *Sustainable Peacebuilding Strategies. Sustainable Peacebuilding Operations in Nakuru County, Kenya: Contribution to the Catholic Justice and Peace Commission (CJPC)*, 2020, 195pp. ISBN: 978-2-88931-331-0

Mary Rose-Claret Ogbuehi, *The Struggle for Women Empowerment Through Education*, 2020, 410pp. ISBN: 978-2-88931-363-1

Nestor Engone Elloué, *La justice climatique restaurative: Réparer les inégalités Nord/Sud*, 2020, 198pp. ISBN 978-2-88931-379-2

African Law Series

Ghislain Patrick Lessène, *Code international de la détention en Afrique*, 2013, 620pp. ISBN: 978-2-940428-70-0

D. Brian Dennison/ Pamela Tibihikirra-Kalyegira (eds.), *Legal Ethics and Professionalism. A Handbook for Uganda*, 2014, 400pp. ISBN 978–2–88931–011–1

Pascale Mukonde Musulay, *Droit des affaires en Afrique subsaharienne et économie planétaire*, 2015, 164pp. ISBN: 978–2–88931–044–9

Pascal Mukonde Musulay, *Démocratie électorale en Afrique subsaharienne: Entre droit, pouvoir et argent*, 2016, 209pp. ISBN 978–2–88931–156–9

Pascal Mukonde Musulay, *Droits, libertés et devoirs de la personne et des peuples en droit international africain Tome I Promotion et protection*, 282pp. 2021, ISBN 978-2-88931-397-6

Pascal Mukonde Musulay, *Droits, libertés et devoirs de la personne et des peuples en droit international africain Tome II Libertés, droits et obligations démocratiques*, 332pp. 2021, ISBN 978-2-88931-399-0

Ambroise Katambu Bulambo, *Règlement judiciaire des conflits électoraux. Précis de droit comparé africain*, 2021, 672pp., ISBN 978-2-88931-403-4

David Brian Dennison, *The Status, Rights and Treatment of Persons with Disabilities within Customary Legal Frameworks in Uganda: A Study of Mukono District*, 2021, 355pp. ISBN 978-2-88931-395-2

Osita C. Eze, *African Charter on Rights & Duties Enforcement Mechanisms*, 2021, 412pp. ISBN: 978-2-88931-413-3

This is only selection of our latest publications, to view our full collection please visit:

www.globethics.net/publications